Trials of the C1

By Gregory D. Yancey, Esq.

"Hell is empty and all the devils are here!"

TRIALS OF THE CHRISTIAN LAWYER
By Gregory D. Yancey, Esq.

Printed in the United States of America

ISBN-13: 978-0692378014
Published by:

The Fighting Lawyer, LLC™
Columbia, Maryland
www.TheFightingLawyer.com

Edited by Nicole Wilson
Cover and Chapter art prepared by Pross Comics
Photography by The Documentist, Jon Armstrong

For more information go to **www.TheFightingLawyer.com** or follow *The Fighting Lawyer* on: Facebook, Twitter, Instagram, and YouTube.

Foreword

Every lawyer is tempted not only to eat forbidden fruit, but also to become the snake. Have you ever been surrounded by pure evil? Have you ever experienced hell on earth? Have you ever been in a situation where there is no presence of God except within you?

The legal profession merits the moniker of "the noble profession" due to the heightened conscientiousness and policing of ethical standards. Attorneys follow rules to represent a client, to bill a client, to try a case, to advertise, and to even stay licensed. For the most part, they submit to the rules of ethics and a professional code of conduct; however, when more than one person in a situation gives into darkness the light gets buried.

This devotion serves as a reminder to always look toward the hills from "whence cometh our help" and the inevitability of God's promises of reward and punishment. This is your survival guide in the midst of the battle when there are no choirs singing your praise. God may appear to be hidden or even powerless to injustice. However, we know that every knee shall bow and every tongue shall confess that Jesus Christ is Lord. "Every knee" includes the enemy and all of his followers.

The apostles found elation in being worthy of suffering for the gospel. The apostles found peace and strength through uncompromised faith. *The Trials of the Christian Lawyer* extend beyond the courtroom and the boardroom to a struggle which is neither with flesh nor blood, but spiritual warfare.

As you read each daily devotional, please do not get caught up in the entertainment value of a particular story. Take time to reflect upon:

1) the scripture that is presented,
2) the questions at the end of the devotional, and
3) the place where the Holy Spirit is telling you to go to next in your Christian journey.

Whether you are an attorney or you work in another faith challenging profession, use this devotional to reveal His glory and truth through your **t.r.i.a.l.s**.

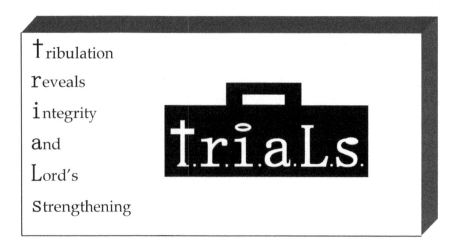

ACKNOWLEDGEMENTS

I give all glory and honor to my Lord and Savior, **Jesus Christ**. The Wonderful Counselor was betrayed, humiliated, denied, beaten, and crucified for me. The world's greatest lawyer made the case for humanity, made the case for justice, made the case for grace and mercy, and made the case for a sinner like me.

I thank God for my beautiful wife, **Jewell Yancey,** who stood by me and with me through every trial. You are the love of my life and the life of my love!

I hold **Cora** and **Gregory** as my inspirations to see a better world and to be a brighter light within it. You are God's gift that neither I nor this world could ever truly deserve. I will always be amazed, proud, and humbled to watch you grow in Him.

I honor my parents/heroes, **Ronald** and **Sheila Yancey** for the seeds that they sowed and the weeds that they pulled to cultivate me in the truth of the gospel.

I extend gratitude to **Mary Day** for her endless wisdom and for advising me to write this devotional.

Disclaimers

The people and events depicted in this devotional are fictional. Any resemblance to actual people and actual events is unintended and merely coincidental.

The devotional contains quotes of famous and historical individuals to encourage further thought on various topics. The reference to the quote does not imply that the quoted person endorses this book or any of the subject matter contained within this devotional. To understand the quoted person's specific intent and meaning, one would have to study the exact context and circumstances in which the quote was articulated.

TABLE OF CONTENTS

CHAPTER 7 - Trials of the Spirit 293

CHAPTER 1

TRIALS OF THE TEN COMMANDMENTS

"For this is the love of God:
that we keep his commandments.
And his commandments
do not weigh us down."
1 John 5:3 NET

Day 1

No Other Gods

"You shall have no other gods before me."
Exodus 20:3 - NIV

"To think of all the things I did for the staff. Times I opened a line of credit to make payroll when *no one* was bringing in money, but me! I should've fired those leeches a long time ago!" Sullivan Keating griped to Crystal for the tenth time in one night. Crystal, his loyal secretary, stood by the captain as he sank with the ship known as the Law Offices of Sullivan C. Keating.

The eviction had been set for tomorrow morning, yet Sullivan's denial prevented him from removing his possessions from the office until the eleventh hour. For two months, Crystal worked without pay. She tried to convince him to file for bankruptcy and to start over with new partners, but Sullivan stayed the course into an iceberg of insolvency.

Crystal snuck a quick glance at her phone to check the time and for any text messages from her husband. The clock on her phone flashed 10:37 pm. She had proven herself to be a loyal employee and friend; in fact, she had boxed up more than her fair share of Sullivan's property. It was time to leave. It was time to live her life. With a quick hug, she sheepishly whispered, "Bye, Sully."

"Go ahead and leave, just like everyone else," yelled Sullivan as Crystal picked up her purse and walked out of the senior partner's office into the lobby. For no explicable reason, a compelling mood or better yet a controlling spirit prevented her from leaving the building. The irresistible spirit convinced her to tell Sullivan to move on and to stop blaming others. As she re-entered Sullivan's office, Crystal shrieked. Sullivan Cornelius Keating, the once famed trial lawyer, now sat in an empty office scratching his head with a semi-automatic handgun.

"Sully, what are you doing?" Crystal asked.

"I went through two divorces for this firm, missed out on half of my kid's childhood and little league games to give my associates cases to work and advanced their careers, but I get nothing!" Sullivan ranted.

Crystal could not stomach the complaining anymore and interjected, "Sully, your god is dead – it's time to believe in the real one!" Sullivan wanted a listening ear instead of a fiery tongue. Crystal's lecture distracted him from noticing that she dialed 911 on her mobile phone and turned down the volume. Sullivan's crying drowned out the repeated "Hello? Hello?" voiced by the puzzled 911 dispatcher. The dispatcher soon realized that he would find more answers by listening to the caller instead of talking.

"*Sullivan Keating*, you are not going to *kill* yourself because of this firm. *1615 Sycamore Street* is just an office. Your life is out there!" Crystal chastened while tipping off the dispatcher of her emergency and location. "It's just that your priorities were always wrong. Just look around you. You carefully wrapped your diplomas and labeled the boxes with the firm art, but you just threw family photos and your son's drawing into any old box!" Crystal shrieked. The secretary's tirade chronicled years of working for an excessive boss who rented more office space than he could afford, hired people to fill office spaces that he could not pay, and then worked too many hours seeking business that did not exist.

Sullivan Keating worshipped his firm and placed his degree, name, profession, possessions, lifestyle, finances, and everything else above God. Sullivan realized that it was more important to focus on the fact that he abandoned God than on the people who abandoned him. The renowned attorney pushed the gun back into the desk drawer and sobbed. Crystal breathed a sigh of relief and opened the front door to let police officers and Emergency Medical Technicians into the office. She thanked God in a short prayer that the 911 dispatcher had picked up on her cues.

The First Commandment, by its placement alone, emphasizes God as our number one priority. The life of Moses, as revealed in Exodus through Deuteronomy, pronounces the downfall of a nation that struggled with idols. Moses' greatest battles were against Israelites, not Pharaoh.

Even as the great prophet stood on Mt. Sinai with God, his people turned to a golden calf. The Lord, then, made an incredible offer to Moses. The Lord indicated that he would wipe out the Israelites and make Moses a leader of a powerful nation with even more people.[1] Moses declined the offer and pled for his people.

---

[1] **Deuteronomy 9:14**

Moses later regretted pleading for the people who caused him to lose fellowship with the Father, who plotted his murder in rebellion, and who were prophesied to turn to idols even after his death. The book of Deuteronomy is filled with Moses' warnings against idolatry along with a sad prophecy that the people will still fall.[2] How could these people forget God after He delivered them from so much? They saw the miracles and even heard His voice, yet they turned their hearts from him.

We are susceptible to the same folly of the Israelite backsliders and Sullivan Keating, if not more, whenever we put anything before God.

We must bow to Him daily, present a sacrificial offering daily, read scripture daily, pray to Him daily, praise and worship daily, and keep our attention on Him daily to ensure that we place "no other gods before Him". Tear down the idols in your life and help others to tear down their idols as well.

His commandments do not weigh us down, they anchor us. We spend time in prayer, in the scriptures, in worship, and in fellowship because His ways are higher and greater than our ways. Be faithful in your marriage to Him.

---

[2] **Deuteronomy 31:29**

CROSS EXAMINATION – *Examined by the Cross*

1. *What are the idols in your life?*
2. *Do you have an altar to God? An altar can be a place where you pray to God. It can be a place where you sacrifice your time, treasure, or talents for Him.*
3. *What is your altar to God?*
4. *Where is your altar?*
5. *What efforts do you make to keep Him first?*

"Two cities have been formed by two loves:
the earthly city by the love of self, leading to contempt of God and
the heavenly city by the love of God, leading to contempt of self.
The former glorifies in itself, the latter in the Lord. . .
These cities are the communities of men."
St. Augustine

Day 2

No Other Image

**"Thou shall not make unto thee *any* graven image,
or any likeness *of any thing* that is in heaven above,
or that is in the earth beneath,
or that *is* in the water under the earth."
Exodus 20:4 in part– KJV**

The secretaries congregated near Joan's desk in anticipation of the big reveal. Joan, the office manager, took exceptional pride and delight in coming up with the annual holiday party theme. In prior years, she selected: a casino night, a red party in which everyone had to dress in red, a toga party, a superhero costume party, and even a pajama party which elicited several racy outfits. The staff gleefully crowded around Joan's desk in wonder. Joan soon pulled leis and tikis from the large cardboard box to the laughter of the secretaries.

"A luau, yes!" yelled Betty as she joked about how some of the attorneys became more human after a few "adult beverages." Joan scanned the room to feast on the joy that she brought to her co-workers. Office managers primarily deal with staff in contentious circumstances, so the holiday party allowed Joan to interact with the staff in pleasant circumstances.

News of Joan's great unveiling trickled down the hallway to the delight of the attorneys. Everyone appeared happy except for Theresa, a junior associate. Theresa looked into Joan's box, and then walked away with an unmistakably disappointed shrug of her shoulders.

"What's the matter, Mother? Let me guess. You have something against luaus, too," mocked Joan. Theresa garnered the name, "Mother" one evening when the partners and the associates left the office to go to a strip club. After Theresa asked them where they were going, they invited her to join them. Two other female attorneys actually joined the excursion and teased Theresa for being so uptight. The attorneys nicknamed her "Mother Theresa" for being too prudish for a strip club. The taunts later carried over to the secretarial staff as well.

"Luaus are fun. I like the food, the music, and even the dancing. . . I just don't like tikis, that's all," said Theresa. Theresa tried to avoid a confrontation with Joan out of fear of dampening everyone's excitement, but she felt cornered.

Betty quickly interjected her beliefs of tolerance, "They're just decorations for a party. That's why I like my church. We don't get so bent out of shape about things. Tikis are supposedly for good luck. It's just for fun."

"You can say what you want, but these are images of false gods. Do you see the irony of honoring the birth of Christ with tiki idols?" Theresa asked.

Theresa became the butt of several jokes at the holiday party. Whenever a person lit a tiki candle, drank from a tiki cup, or even bowed to the large wooden tiki idol near the karaoke machine, someone had to say, "Forgive us, Mother."

Betty brought red plastic cups to the party stating that she did not want the Holy Mother to be offended. Theresa could not help but to notice that Betty and a few of the others sipped soft drinks from the red plastic cups. They must have felt uneasy about the tikis. Theresa did not mind the ridicule as much if it meant that she had taken a stand for God and empowered others to do so too.

"Thank you, Lord. You always make a way out for those who honor you," Theresa softly prayed.

CROSS EXAMINATION - *Examined by the Cross*

1. *God has no tolerance for idols. See Exodus 34:13-14*
2. *Do you come into contact with images of false gods? Astrology? Tiki's? Tarot cards? Other religions? Mythology?*
3. *How do you respond when you see images of other religions?*
4. *In which circumstances should a Christian be respectful and tolerant of other religions and in which circumstances should they take a stand like Gideon? See Judges 6:25.*

"Let us remove the ignorance and darkness
that spreads like a mist over our sight,
and let us get a vision of the true God."
Clement of Alexandria

Day 3

ḣoly ıs Thy Naṁe

**"Thou shalt not take the name of the Lord
thy God in vain; for the Lord will not hold him
guitless that taketh his name in vain."
Exodus 20:7 - KJV**

" Jesus Christ! I wish clients would read my *(4 - letter word)* emails!" vented Tony in the break room. His client had submitted an incomplete set of documents, now he would have to explain to opposing counsel why certain records were missing. Other attorneys and paralegals soon piled on their complaints about incompetent clients and the frustration they experience when people "just don't read." Brenda, the senior partner's secretary happened to be rinsing out her I ♥ Jesus coffee mug in the break room sink as the veins in Tony's neck continued to surge.

Whenever Tony yelled "Jesus Christ", Brenda immediately shouted "The name above all names, Hallelujah!" Although Brenda did not attend law school, she knew twice as much about the firm, the partners of the firm, and the court system in the county. The partners would sooner fire the entire staff than to see her leave. All of the associates, including Tony, respected and feared her.

"I was just telling them about the Walker case and how. . .," began the young attorney feeling judged.

"Jesus Christ isn't a curse word. I'm sure God also gets frustrated with us when we *just don't read* the Bible, but He shows us grace," Brenda continued. Tony apologized for offending her beliefs, but Brenda emphasized that this was more than an offense to her beliefs. She genuinely feared for his wellbeing and the tone that it set for others to blaspheme Jesus Christ. Some of the staff left the break room to avoid a "religious conversation" while others left because they had enjoyed Tony's venting.

Over the next year, Tony occasionally slipped and used the Savior's name in vain. After each blasphemous utterance, Brenda shouted "The name above names. Hallelujah!" Ironically, the staff felt more uncomfortable with Brenda's praise than Tony's sacrilege. Eventually, Tony used the name of Jesus only in prayer and only to give honor and glory to God.

The Third Commandment warns against irreverence towards the Lord and irreverence to His name. Do not use the Lord's name in vain. We use the name in vain when we use it as profanity, but we also use it in vain with casual terms like OMG! and TGIF in which we do not respect the holiness in a name that our forefathers even feared to say aloud.

The Lord promises that He will not hold anyone "guiltless" who takes His name in vain.

CROSS EXAMINATION - Examined by the Cross

1. *Why is it a sin to use God's name in vain?*
2. *Is it possible to use the Lord's name in vain even when saying common church terminology like: "My Lord", "Help me, Jesus", "God, bless you", and "the Lord told me" if a person doesn't mean it?*
3. *Is it possible to use the Lord's name in vain while singing Christian music if your heart isn't in it?*
4. *Is it our responsibility to correct a nonbeliever for using the Lord's name in vain if they don't think of it as being offensive?*
5. *Do you consider terms like OMG and T.G.I.F to be using the Lord's name in vain? Do you think people are thinking about God when they say the terms?*

"But to take God's name in vain is not just a matter of words
–it's also about thoughts and deeds. . .
To call God "Lord" and disobey him is to take his name in vain.
To call God "Father" and be filled with anxiety and
doubts is to deny his name."
John Stott

Day 4

KEEPING THE SABBATH

"Remember the sabbath day, to keep it holy."
Exodus 20:8 - KJV

This would be the fifth weekend in a row that Thema missed church to work in the firm. There were always briefs to write, billing records to prepare, or even clients to meet who were unable to meet during normal work hours. Thema loved the fact that she could get a recording of her church service and listen to it later. Sometimes, Thema would even watch the service online from the office.

In today's service, Pastor Dennis preached about the Sabbath and the reason God rested. "God did not need to rest. God only needed to provide an example for us to set aside a time of remembrance and holiness. What could you possibly be doing that's more important than worshipping God?" questioned the pastor rhetorically.

The pastor warned the congregation to avoid two extremes: the extreme of worshipping the Sabbath more than God and the extreme of disregarding the Sabbath and the opportunity to worship God.

The pastor preached, "In Luke 14:3, Jesus told the Pharisees that God created the Sabbath for man and not vice versa when he questioned them on the legality of healing on a holy day. Some of us have to do God's work on the Sabbath."

He went on to preach that some people *have* to work otherwise there would be no police, no doctors, and no firefighters available on the Sabbath. Pastor Dennis laughed while stating that there would be no preaching on the Sabbath if pastors rested.

"It's okay to work on the Sabbath if you *have* to. The question at the end of the day is who is your God? Who do you make time for? Where is your priority? Are you seeking a true worship experience or are you fitting Him into your schedule?" preached the pastor.

Warm tears streamed down Thema's face. She was proud of herself for at least tuning into the service, but she felt guilty for missing the fellowship of believers. She missed lending her voice to praise and worship, seeing people face-to-face, and even giving the service her full attention as opposed to listening to it while typing pleadings. Thema resolved in her heart that the Sabbath would no longer be a make-up work day for her, but a day of rest and worship.

As Thema avoided working on the Sabbath over the next few months, she became more focused during the work week and better organized. She felt connected to God and found constant rest and renewal every weekend. Thema realized that by keeping the Sabbath holy, she remained holy.

CROSS EXAMINATION – *Examined by the Cross*

1. *Do you honor God on the Sabbath? If so, how do you honor Him? Some people go to church, some listen to worship music, some read the Bible, some abstain from certain activities, etc.*
2. *Between the two extremes of worshipping the Sabbath and ignoring the Sabbath, where do you fall? Do you have this balanced?*
3. *What is your Sabbath? Is it a day of the week? Do you observe it every day at a particular time?*

"And God in his goodness has called us to live out the
Christian life together, as our mutual love
and care reflect the love and care of God.
Relationships imply commitment in the world.
Surely they imply no less in the church.
He never meant our growth to occur alone on an island but
with and through one another."
Mark Dever

Day 5

ᕼonor Thy ᕈarents

**"Honor your father and your mother,
so that you may live long in the land
the Lord your God is giving you."
Exodus 20:12- NIV**

Thomas hated it when a client left multiple voicemails in one day. He had been in court all afternoon. Whether clients left one message or three, he would still return the call in the order in which he received them. Nevertheless, Rosetta Matulka sounded desperate regarding her mother's fading health. Thomas quickly returned the phone call to learn that Rosetta needed a will prepared for her mother. Stomach cancer had recently sentenced her mother, Liza Matulka, to hospice and there seemed to be little hope for a miraculous healing. Rosetta complained that she needed a will and various powers of attorneys drafted immediately in order to make necessary medical and financial decisions for her mother.   Rosetta had lived with her mother for the last eight years prior to placing Liza into hospice.

After her father died, Rosetta assumed more responsibility for the care of her mother and moved into her home. Her older sister, Monica, resided barely twenty miles north of Liza and Rosetta, yet she only visited on major holidays. Monica's priorities rested with her immediate family and career.

Instead of going home early or billing more hours in the office, Thomas returned the phone call. He quickly agreed to meet Rosetta at the hospice. The off-the-clock attorney listened to Liza's complaints about the burning in her stomach. The nurses commended Rosetta for her care and attention to her mother's cancer treatment. Some even joked that Rosetta deserved a nurse's uniform. Thomas prayed silently to himself that the Lord would ease Liza's pain either through a healing or by calling her to her heavenly home. He, then, asked Rosetta and the nurses to leave the room so he could speak to Liza privately. Rosetta reluctantly exited.

Thomas questioned Liza about the terms of her will and whether she wanted a power of attorney. Liza gushed on and on about Rosetta's care and attentiveness, but she had no idea about what to do with her home. She feared that if she gave equal ownership of the home to both daughters, then Monica could force a sale and leave Rosetta homeless. She feared that Monica would feel unloved if she gave the entire home to Rosetta.

"Ms. Matulka, I can put language in the will stating that your daughters share ownership of the property, but Rosetta can live in it and make the final decision on whether to sell it or to maintain it," Thomas offered. Suddenly it became clear to Thomas that Rosetta pressured Liza about inheriting the entire house. Liza decided to leave everything to Rosetta out of fear of losing her daughter or, even worse, finding out that Rosetta never loved her and only wanted the house.

Now, Thomas felt sick in his stomach too. He had to draft a will for a dying woman under duress by her primary caretaker. Both daughters disgusted him. Monica dishonored her mother by showing little concern about Liza's health. Rosetta dishonored her mother through emotional manipulation in Liza's moment of greatest need.

Thomas left hospice and followed the directives of his client and drafted the will and power of attorney. Within hours, he returned to his client's bedside with a freshly drafted will and power of attorney. Rosetta no longer held the compunction to maintain pretenses and openly commanded Thomas to make further revisions to the will for her mother's jewelry and other effects. Rosetta's evil clearly surfaced.

Thomas wasted precious words of wisdom in advising Rosetta to honor her mother and to think of her mother's needs.

"We have to honor our parents, not just before man, but before God. When we dishonor our parents, we dishonor the God who put them over us," concluded Thomas. By the end of the week, Liza went to be with the Lord and Rosetta became her only heir.

CROSS EXAMINATION – *Examined by the Cross*

1. *What are some of the ways that you honor your parents?*
2. *What are some of the ways that you dishonor them?*
3. *Have your parents gone to be with the Lord?*
4. *Is it possible to honor and dishonor your parents who are no longer alive?*

Day 6

MURDER BY OMISSION

"Thou shalt not kill."
Exodus 20:13 - KJV

"So Mr. Sevics, you're the attorney – tell us how to keep the bulls-eye off our backs," ordered Shikha Patikh the Chief Operating Officer ("COO") of Foxhen Motors. In a meeting with in-house counsel, the COO disclosed the fact that .3% of their cars had a design defect that resulted in fatalities in high impact collisions. The statistics suggested that Foxhen customers faced greater odds of dying from a drunk driver than from a product malfunction; nevertheless, upper management and the quality control team knew of a serious problem.

"We reduce liability by making safer cars," opined Reginald Sevics as he offered an obvious solution. The table became increasingly hostile as people acknowledged the impracticality of making a 100% safe vehicle. Even when there are no design defects, there is a possibility for a manufacturing error with domestic or foreign assembly lines.

The quality control team rifled off statistics to show that people were more likely to die from choking on peanuts, slipping in a bathtub, or even getting hit by a drunk driver than dying from the engine defect.

"Are we going to disclose this defect? Are we going to warn people?" asked Sevics directly pleading to their consciences.

"Do you want a product recall? You want to lose billions of dollars? Have federal investigations? Deal with frivolous lawsuits? Lose credibility with our investors? Lose thousands of employees to offset our losses? Think about all the good that we do through Foxhen Motors Cares!" ranted Patikh becoming increasingly frustrated with the advice that the company's attorney offered.

Reginald had to admit that the Foxhen Motors Cares nonprofit entity provided scholarships to so many in need. He also thought about the environmental good that their engineers implemented by reducing exhaust emissions. He could not give sound advice when any decision would cause some suffering. If he blew the whistle, he could save thousands of lives from car accidents; however, he would also cost tens of thousands, if not hundreds of thousands, of jobs.

"We have blood on our hands if we sell unsafe vehicles," Reginald warned.

"So we're murderers? People knowingly take a risk any time they step into a car, take medication, even get out of bed in the morning. We aren't murderers if 99.7% of our customers live happier lives driving affordable cars that are reliable 100% of the time. The remaining .3% are more likely to die from texting or speeding than from our defects," challenged Eugene Weathersby from Quality Assurance.

Reginald bought into the argument, but struggled all night over the fact that two people had recently died due to an engine explosion. The accidents in Topeka, Kansas and in Green Bay, Wisconsin appeared to the public as isolated incidents, but in-house counsel and upper management knew the common thread. Reginald knew the cause of the malfunction. Was he a murderer? Was he an accomplice? Over the next few years, Reginald's conscience could no longer tolerate the Foxhen Motors cover-ups and denials as more deaths occurred in the United States and overseas.

Reginald violated attorney-client confidentiality by writing anonymous letters to the families of the victims. He further betrayed his employer's trust by writing unsigned letters to local authorities and watchdog groups about the cause of the engine failures.

Reginald eventually resigned from Foxhen Motors because of his imploding conscience. He had been wrong at every turn. The in-house counselor betrayed the American people by covering up design defects; in addition, he betrayed his company by exposing confidentially obtained information. Despite his serious ethical lapses, he retired from the company feeling less like a murderer.

Murder goes beyond a physical taking of a life. The scriptures warn us that God will judge us for even having a murderous heart and indifference to life[3]. In Kings 21:19, the Lord called Ahab out for murder. Even though Ahab never laid a hand on Naboth, he allowed an innocent man to be defamed and killed for a piece of property.

CROSS EXAMINATION – *Examined by the Cross*

1. *Why is murder a sin?*
2. *How have you murdered through anger, resentment, or even apathy?*
3. *Have you committed murder or been complicit to deaths caused by an employer or client?*
4. *Does this commandment affect your views on political issues such as: war, capital punishment, abortion, euthanasia, health care, poverty, or any other issue? Should it?*

---

[3] **1 John 3:15**

Day 7

Maꞧꞧıaɢꞓ UNaõulꞓꞧaꞓõ

"Thou shalt not commit adultery."
Exodus 20:14 - KJV

Curtis yawned like a lion. His eyes watered from fatigue as they strained through volumes of the state annotated code. It was already 7:20 pm and he envisioned another three hours in the firm library before heading home to his family.

"Curtis. . . I mean Mr. Swansfield. I was thinking about going to law school, but I don't know if I have the GPA or LSAT scores to get in," interrupted Jennifer Darounos, a legal secretary recently transferred to his floor. Curtis welcomed the interruption from his tedious reading of state procedural regulations. He immediately explained the path that he took to get into law school.

As he offered his best advice, Curtis soon realized that Jennifer had no interest in becoming an attorney. The increasingly flirtatious co-worker quickly offered to pick up some Chinese food and to help him prepare for trial. Jennifer advised him about the importance of staying relaxed before a big trial while gently dropping a hand on one of Curtis' shoulders in circular massaging patterns.

"Shhh, can you hear that?" asked Curtis as Jennifer's flirting became more blatant. Jennifer tried to listen, but could not catch what Curtis was hearing. Pointing to his ring, Curtis said, "Listen again, it's saying '*He's unavailable!*'" Jennifer left the office embarrassed, saddened, and furious with Curtis.

Curtis could have let her down in a more polite way, but he wanted to drive home the point that Jennifer had disrespected him, herself, and his wife. He did not want to shoot her down politely only to be tempted at another time. Work was no longer possible this evening as Curtis' anger boiled. The encounter upset him far more than Jennifer because he had more to lose. Jennifer's temptation could have led him to hurt his wife, Amy, and his three children.

Amy trusted him to work long hours to help their family. They stood together at the dedication of their youngest daughter to the Lord, and they stood together when their oldest daughter was baptized. What kind of example would Curtis set for his son if he cheated on his wife? How could he ever do such a thing to the God who blessed him with his job and his family? Why would Jennifer do something that could cost him everything he had?

Curtis discussed the encounter with his wife and then later shared it with the managing partner. Even though he had done nothing wrong and never considered sleeping with Jennifer, he preferred to have accountability on and off the job to ensure that he never stumbled. Curtis also disclosed the truth to the managing partner out of fear that Jennifer could lie and tell others that he had made advances towards her.

The partner believed Curtis overreacted to Jennifer's advances and should have taken it as a compliment. Curtis disagreed based on his understanding of the Seventh Commandment. God created woman and marriage so that man would not be alone. He argued that adultery violates the sacred covenant of marriage and robs both participants of God's blessings and gift. Curtis fought too hard to keep his marriage and his witness undefiled. "As marriages fall, families fall, communities fall, and nations fall," said Curtis.

Curtis maintained that he did not want Jennifer to lose her job, but he wanted another person to share with her the importance of respecting marriage and respecting herself. Curtis made a convincing argument which eventually led the partner to reach out to Jennifer.

"Marriage is to be held in honor among all,
and the marriage bed is to be undefiled;
for fornicators and adulterers God will judge."
Hebrews 13:4 - NIV

<u>CROSS EXAMINATION</u> – *Examined by the Cross*

1. *Have you ever experienced the pitfalls of adultery in your marriage or observed the effects of adultery in other marriages?*
2. *What steps have you taken to protect your marriage or the marriage of others?*
3. *Did Curtis overreact to Jennifer's flirting? Read Genesis 39.*
4. *Some people have "open marriages". Can a spouse give you permission to violate a covenant with God?*
5. *Some people believe that flirting is "necessary" in certain business situations. When at least one of the people involved is married, does flirting equal adultery? Read Matthew 5:8.*

"Sin will always take you further than you wanted to go and cost you more than you wanted to pay."
Tony Evans

Day 8

No Such Thing As Theft

"Thou shalt not steal."
Exodus 20:15 KJV

"Look Frazier, I'm giving you a heads up. This thing is over. Apparently, my client just decided to accept your initial settlement offer," said Seanathan Moody. Seanathan's assurance ended *Smith vs. Hozier Pharmaceuticals*, a hotly contested breach of contract case in the early stages. Seanathan's client, Mason Smith, filed suit claiming that he did not receive royalties for the heart medication that he invented as a partner of Hozier Pharmaceuticals.

The multi-million dollar law suit drew near an end simply due to a freak accident. Mr. Smith's home burned down because of an old dryer. The insurance company refused to cover his loss because he had left the house to grocery shop while the dryer had been running. Without a home, Mr. Smith no longer had the finances or the intestinal fortitude to proceed with his lawsuit against Hozier so he agreed to settle his claim for a lesser amount.

Although happy for his client, Frazier began to panic. The sole practitioner relied on this case to pay his mortgage and office overhead for awhile. He had also neglected marketing efforts thus failing to bring in new business over the last few months. Frazier thought about telling his client the good news, then decided to wait. Anticipating a long trial, the experienced attorney had already spent some of the twenty thousand dollar retainer without having done much work on the case.

"Until we have something in writing, there is no deal," Frazier thought as he started drafting discovery documents to request evidence and witness names from opposing counsel. The now rattled attorney decided to burn as much of the retainer as he possibly could.

Frazier, then, directed his paralegal to research case law on the enforceability of employer-employee royalty agreements while he spent several hours researching work-for-hire patents. Frazier accumulated more billable hours on the case over the next three days, than he had over the prior three weeks. The sole practitioner finally informed his client that Mr. Smith agreed to settle the case a week after his conversation with opposing counsel.

Frazier billed Hozier based on his financial needs as opposed to his client's legal needs. Even though Frazier provided legal services, the work was unnecessary. He stole from his client.

God abhors theft because He stands for justice. Theft hurts others. In addition to the actual loss of money, theft sets a false example that godlessness rules. Theft causes people to distrust God and leads them to take matters into their own hands. Even though Frazier used the money he stole for the good purpose of paying his bills, he still succumbed to a form of *lust* and *pride*. He succumbed to *lust* because he desired something that was outside of God's will for his life. God does not want his children to steal. Frazier succumbed to *pride* because his pride convinced him that he knew better than God. Pride leads one to think that he or she is entitled to things that God does not provide us.

Hozier Pharmaceuticals never noticed the theft, but God saw everything. Divine justice never fails. In the grand scheme of things, there is no such thing as theft. Everyone will pay, at some point, for anything and everything that is stolen.

CROSS EXAMINATION – *Examined by the Cross*

1. *Have you ever been a victim of theft?*
2. *What tangible things have you ever stolen?*
3. *What are the intangible things that you have stolen? (Ex. People steal ideas, credit, time, joy, identity, etc.)*
4. *Is it theft to buy something only for the purpose of using it and returning it?*
5. *In your own words, describe how theft equates to rebellion against God.*
6. *Do you agree with the idea that there is no such thing as theft since we'll pay for it in the end?*
   How do you feel about the fact that even if God punishes Frazier, his client still suffered?
7. *If God owns everything, does that make Him a victim in every theft?*
8. *Theft = coveting + lust + pride + idolatry*

"When our deepest desire is not the things of God, or a favor from God, but God Himself, we cross a threshold."
Max Lucado

Day 9

fALSE WITNESS

**"Thou shalt not bear false witness
against thy neighbour[4]."
Exodus 20:16 - KJV**

"I don't get involved in these things," stammered the pediatrician. Dr. Harrison knew that Eric Johnson was a great father to Cassidy and a great husband to Amanda Johnson. He felt sorry for Mr. Johnson, but did not want to be involved in a court hearing. Amanda cheated on her husband, left the marital home, hired a divorce attorney, and was now making allegations of child abuse to get custody of the children.

Amanda brought Cassidy to his office a week ago. During the appointment, Cassidy told Dr. Harrison that she had scraped her knees from a fall at recess. He listened as Amanda tried to pressure Cassidy to say that her father had abused her.

"She couldn't get Cassidy to lie in your office last week, so she took her to Child Protective Services yesterday and pressured her to lie to them. You know this is wrong! Why won't you go to court and tell the truth?" asked attorney Marcia Valdez.

---

[4] This is the King James Version spelling of the word "neighbor".

"I don't want to be dragged into court every time parents get a divorce. I would lose half my practice for siding with one over the other. I could also expect complaints to the medical board from the parent that loses!" argued Dr. Harrison. He cited the fact that the medical records should be sufficient since it indicated that there was no finding of abuse.

Marcia erupted, "The medical records just say that there was no finding of abuse. It doesn't say that Amanda tried to get her daughter to lie about an innocent man." Dr. Harrison remained unmoved by the fact that Mr. Johnson could be labeled a child abuser based on the unsubstantiated testimony of an opportunistic divorcee.

As Marcia retreated from the office in defeat, she noticed a Ten Commandments paperweight on the receptionist's desk. "I guess you don't mind breaking the commandment about bearing false witness," Marcia said as she lifted the paperweight of the two stone tablets.

"What are you talking about? Bearing false witness? I'm not *bearing any witness*," remarked Dr. Harrison.

"If you don't speak up, then you are saying that Mr. Johnson is guilty of child abuse. You are also saying that Mrs. Johnson did nothing wrong even though she tried to force a young girl to lie in your office. You are bearing false witness and guilty of the same lie that she will tell in court. God isn't happy with lies of commission or omission," relayed Marcia as she placed the paperweight into Dr. Harrison's hands.

The next morning, Marcia received a call from Dr. Harrison's secretary to confirm the trial date and time.

"If a person sins because he does not speak up
when he hears a public charge to testify
regarding something he has seen or learned about,
he will be held responsible."
Leviticus 5:1 - NIV

CROSS EXAMINATION – *Examined by the Cross*

1. What are the ways that you bear false witness either by commission or omission?
2. What are the ways that you have seen attorneys bear false witness?
3. Is it lying when attorneys withhold facts?
4. Is it lying when attorneys shake their heads and feign disdain while a witness testifies truthfully?
5. Is it lying to remain silent when people spread gossip and false reports?

Day 10

COVENANT AGAINST COVETING

**"Thou shalt not covet thy neighbour's house . . .
nor any thing that *is* thy neighbour's[5]."
Exodus 20:17 - KJV**

Milan could not help being envious of Jeff Leopold, the youngest associate to ever make partner in his firm. Jeff wore designer clothes, married an attractive dynamic woman, and had family photos that looked even better than the sample photos that came with the frames. As Milan reviewed his son's college tuition bill for the semester, he imagined Jeff Leopold paying all four years of his son's tuition with one payment.

Milan could not imagine ever making partner. His wife, Alfreda, flopped like a fish out of water at firm networking events. Alfreda had become increasingly conscientious about her grammatical errors when in the presence of attorneys. Milan often blushed from embarrassment from her mistakes and attempts to sound sophisticated.

---

[5] This is the King James Version spelling of the word "neighbor".

This made Alfreda even more nervous and awkward. Sometimes, Milan wondered if she held him back too. Alfreda was nothing like Jeff's wife, Florencia. Florencia Leoppold, a noted federal judge and constitutional scholar, knew how to work every room with brilliance, charm, and humor.

Jeff clearly had the good life. Photos of the partner shaking hands with political leaders and celebrities decorated his office. Within a day's notice, Jeff could catch a flight to any place in the world and be comfortable meeting with a great dignitary or CEO of a Fortune 500 company.

"What's wrong with you, Milan? It's wrong to covet other people! You should appreciate the things that God has given you and celebrate the things that He has blessed others. Alfreda is wonderful. Covetousness leads to idolatry, ungratefulness, pride, lust, and sin," Milan lectured himself. No matter how hard Milan tried to gather his thoughts, his focus inevitably snapped back to the wonderful life of Jeff Leopold.

After checking the bank account balance online, Milan wrote the check for his son's tuition. The check would empty all but two hundred dollars from the account. Milan became so angry that he knocked a binder off of his desk. Hearing the commotion, Jeff Leopold entered the office and asked if everything was okay.

"I'm sorry, I'm just ticked off! I just spent $13,000 on my son's tuition. I'm just frustrated!" explained Milan to the partner.

"Consider yourself fortunate. I just spent over thirty thousand dollars to replace a wrecked car and another forty thousand dollars on legal fees. Don't get me started on the medical bills!" griped Leopold. Within seconds, the partner disclosed his son's pending manslaughter case resulting from a drunk driving accident. His seventeen year old son, Neil, killed a young mother after graduation while driving his graduation gift. The passengers in his vehicle also sustained severe injuries. Jeff cried about the thought of his son spending the next few decades in jail. He also discussed the haunting shame and countless hours spent apologizing to the victim's family. The conversation led to other candid revelations.

"Milan, it must be nice to be an employee and to just work in a firm. . . not having to carry salaries and not having people hate you when they don't get bonuses at the end of the year. I don't even get to see my family except on vacations and then we're trying to get to know each other again," Jeff confessed about the people he left behind while climbing the ladder of success.

Milan regretted harboring foolish bitterness about his son's college tuition in light of the car accident that ended the life of one mother and ruined the life of one father. Milan's pain paled in comparison to the suffering and pressures that came with the life that he coveted. The amazing life of Jeff Leopold no longer seemed so great.

Milan confided to his boss, "God is teaching me to count my blessings. I had a bad habit of coveting others. No matter what blessings we have or problems we have, the only thing that matters is that we have Him." From that day forward, Milan made a covenant with God not to covet.

CROSS EXAMINATION – *Examined by the Cross*

1. *Why is coveting a sin?*
2. *Who did Milan sin against due to his coveting?*
3. *Would your opinion of Milan's sin change if Jeff Leopold actually had lived the great life?*
4. *What additional sins do coveting lead to?*
5. *How have you coveted? How do you avoid it?*
6. *Sometimes we measure ourselves by others for motivational purposes. Where do you draw the line between coveting and simply striving for more in your life?*

CHAPTER 2

TRIALS OF WISDOM

"But he who listens to me shall live securely
and will be at ease from the dread of evil."
Proverbs 1:33 NASB

Day 11

hIGhEST AuThORITY

"Do not be wise in your own eyes;
fear the LORD and shun evil."
Proverbs 3:7 - NIV

K eira Scalise made Judge Hiawatha Caza's skin crawl. He could not understand why he disliked her so much. Kiera had a constant scowl on her face. Caza interpreted every gesture of the plaintiff as indication of an air of superiority and an air of entitlement. Most people at least attempt to smile and make eye contact with the judge when the judge speaks, but Keira seemed to still keep a serious grimace on her face. The venerable judge hated it when men stereotyped women as being catty, yet immediately viewed the woman before him as a catty person.

Caza struggled to maintain an open mind in the case, but there was something nagging at him to make him despise the well-dressed petitioner: jealousy. She had more money than he would ever see in a lifetime. He held no sympathy for a millionaire who lived in a mansion and had a nanny.

Keira Scalise claimed that her mansion caught on fire when the children's nanny changed the batteries in a remote control car. The nanny threw the used 9-volt battery into the trashcan. Unbeknownst to the Scalises or to the nanny, sparks emit whenever metal touches the positive and negative end of the rectangular battery. The battery apparently touched something metal in the trash and sparked into a greater fire after touching paper trash.

Unsatisfied with the insurance company's offer of a $50 million dollar settlement for her home, Keira demanded $55 million and that warning labels be placed on all batteries. The multi-millionaire sued her home insurance carrier and the battery manufacturer.

Caza loathed Keira even more after testimony. He could not fathom any difference between 50 million and 55 million dollars. The insurance company accepted responsibility, but the battery manufacturer refused to accept any liability and refused to change its label.

Judge Caza knew from the beginning of testimony that he would enter a $50 million dollar verdict against the insurance company and that he would dismiss the case against the battery manufacturer. He found himself hating Mrs. Scalise for forcing him to endure two days of testimony on a case she deemed to be about "principles."

The 9-volt warning label advised customers to dispose all batteries in an appropriate and safe manner. Caza opined that there was no need for more explicit directions.

The learned judge recognized that his jealous predisposition created a bias against Keira, but he also maintained that Keira's jarring elitist personality made it difficult for anyone to rule in her favor. In an act of pure wisdom and humility, Caza prayed to God for protection from every evil thought that would cause him to rule unfairly against Keira Scalise. He also prayed for protection from any fear that would discourage him from ruling against the plaintiff. The media featured viral footage of the simmering Scalise mansion throughout litigation causing Caza to fear a backlash from the public for siding with a big corporation. Immediately after praying, Caza felt cleansed and freed from hatred and impure thoughts.

For the next three hours, Caza heard the remaining witnesses and reviewed every exhibit without one malicious thought towards Keira. After closing arguments, Judge Caza still dismissed Keira's complaint against the battery company and valued the damages at $50 million dollars; however, he had a clear conscience that the decision was made based on the facts and the law as opposed to any evil thoughts of jealousy or spite.

Keira Scalise scowled as she left the courtroom determined to appeal to a higher authority. Although the learned judge repented for harboring evil thoughts against Mrs. Scalise, Judge Hiawatha "Bright Arrow" Caza remained at peace with his decision since he had already appealed to the highest authority before entering the judgment.

CROSS EXAMINATION - *Examined by the Cross*

1. *Have you ever had an unjustified dislike, hatred, or prejudice that caused you to have evil thoughts?*
2. *How do you take captive every evil thought? See 2 Corinthians 10:5.*
3. *Judge Caza still made the same decision in the end, so why is it relevant that he prayed when making his decision?*
4. *What are some of the evil thoughts that have infiltrated your mind today? How are the thoughts affecting your actions? Are there outward signs of your inward thinking?*

"Never forget that God is able to lift you from fatigue of despair to the buoyancy of hope, and dark and desolate valleys into sunlit paths of inner peace."
Rev. Dr. Martin Luther King, Jr.

Day 12

Unteachable

As Sarah raced frantically through her file cabinets for the *Baskerville* case, Donna Mansfield, the senior partner, knocked on the open door of her office and requested a few minutes to speak. Sarah did not have a few minutes to speak; however, an associate never refused the senior partner. Donna closed the door behind her as she sat in the chair usually filled by a client. Sarah immediately recognized the tone of voice that always led to a reprimand. In the last six months, Sarah had taken on more clients and billed more than any other associate, yet Donna entered her office to chastise her about one unsatisfied client.

"The secretaries informed me that Mr. Brackens has called this office every day this week complaining that you aren't returning his calls. That's inexcusable," lectured the partner.

"It's only Thursday and Mr. Brackens is a *pro bono* client. I have to focus on the *paying* clients right now. Have you seen my billable hours lately? Why are you always on my back? I see you talking to other associates about your family and personal life, but you hound me!" retorted Sarah.

"First and foremost, we do not give poor service to poor people. Poor people are used to being ignored. We walk in excellence here! Secondly, I have a different relationship with other associates because they *listen*. They are teachable. You aren't. You're a parent. If you have one child who is hardheaded and another one who listens, you spend more time disciplining one and sharing more of your heart with the other," concluded Donna.

Donna's words echoed things that Sarah's mother had shared with her over the years. Sarah had become too prideful to listen to people. Her climb up the professional ladder hardened her to any critique. Donna added, "A person who is unteachable forfeits connection to others, to God, and to a prosperous life."

Donna shared a scripture from her mobile phone:

> **"If you had responded to my rebuke,**
> **I would have poured out my heart to you and**
> **made my thoughts known to you."**
> **Proverbs 1:23 NIV**

Donna's high school soccer coach recited that scripture to her when he selected a less skilled teammate to be captain of the team. Despite the fact that Donna was all-State and went on to play in a Division 1 college, the coach picked a captain who remained teachable.

Donna learned that talent meant nothing without humility. This lesson shaped her into becoming teachable and becoming teachable led her to success on and off the soccer field.

Sarah apologized to Donna and later to Mr. Brackens. By accepting chastisement from Donna, Sarah not only learned about the partner's soccer background, but also that her boss had lost a child to cerebral palsy. Her son's cerebral palsy had been linked to lead based paint just like the death of Mr. Brackens' son. Donna gave Sarah a clearer picture of a parent's grief and the reason why the firm accepted lead paint injury *pro bono* cases.

By accepting chastisement from Mr. Brackens, Sarah learned that her client had obtained case research and a paint sample from his former home that proved the landlord's negligence. Sarah soon discovered that the only way to access information and to access another's heart is to remain teachable. By remaining teachable, her relationship with the Lord also soared to new heights.

CROSS EXAMINATION – *Examined by the Cross*

1. Please re-read Proverbs 1:23 - *God desires to pour out His heart and to share His thoughts with us, but He's limited by our willingness to listen.*
2. *We want to talk. We want to be right. We want to be honored, yet, in most cases, we just need to listen and be humble. Are you blocking God from sharing His thoughts with you?*
3. *Do you notice a different level of closeness with people who accept your constructive criticism versus those who do not? How do you respond to unteachable people?*
4. *Are you unteachable?*
5. *How often do you read your Bible?*

"If we are not feeding on the Word, we are not walking after the Spirit, and we will not have victory over the flesh and over sin."
Robert Torrey

Day 13

WISÐOM vs. FOLLY

**"If a wise man goes to court with a fool,
the fool rages and scoffs, and there is no peace."
Proverbs 29:9 - NIV**

"It is frustrating to stand in court and see a reasonable person and a foolish person receive equal courtesy from a judge," stated Adella Daniels to Ted and Ed Sawyers as their frustrations and fears elevated. Adella and her two clients sat in landlord-tenant court for two hours waiting for their case to be called. Some tenants simply admitted that they had a change in financial circumstances and apologized for not paying rent while others used the system to delay their evictions.

The Sawyers regretted becoming landlords two months after leasing a home to Norris and Wendy Matthews. The Matthews started off paying rent late and then stopped paying at all. They ranted and raved about inexistent housing violations to justify their failure to pay rent. The building inspector visited the property after the Matthews claimed that their new HVAC system did not work.

The Matthews had apparently tampered with the system and then claimed that they had no air conditioning in the summer. The couple changed the locks to the home and threatened to call the police on any technician that attempted to repair the HVAC unit. The tenants requested a postponement so they could find an attorney, but they never hired one. The case was postponed a second time, so the judge could get a report from the building inspector. The case was postponed a third time after the judge gave a stern warning to the Matthews to allow the building inspector to enter the property. Each postponement crushed the spirit of the landlords. The Sawyers were not rich; in fact, they owned only one rental property which now proved to be unprofitable. The brothers could not afford to pay the mortgage on the property without receiving rent. They could not afford any more legal fees or another postponement. This was their final plea for justice.

As the judge took opening statements from Adella Daniels and then listened to Norris Matthews' ranting, Ted Sawyers' blood pressure increased. He could not understand how the judge could listen to lies and the truth with equal attention. Ted prayed that the judge was only being polite to the Matthews and not taking their outlandishness seriously.

Ed made it clear that he would stop being reasonable so that decorum justice could work in the landlords' favor. Decorum justice occurs when judges side with the most cantankerous person to prevent a scene, instead of ruling in favor of justice. It can be disheartening when a foolish person receives greater deference from a judge. The Sawyers started to lose heart. Given the opportunity to speak, Ed intended to yell at the Matthews, the judge, and anyone in the courtroom who could hear him. He assured Adella that he would tell the judge his intentions to break the law and throw the tenants out violently if the tenants are not evicted.

Adella whispered to her clients at the trial table, "Some people have the ability to change the atmosphere with their foolishness, with their rage, and with their scoffing. Do not lose heart. You should never conform to the patterns of this world. Never bring unnecessary foolishness, rage, or strife into court for theatrical purposes. Never act like a fool just to get your way." She advised them to continue pleading their case to the highest judge in a court of prayer regardless of the outcome. Ed apologize for giving into his anger and then prayed. The judge awarded the Sawyers possession of their property without even requiring them to testify.

Faith in God assures us that good cannot win by evil means. Faith in God exhibits the wisdom of never trading eternity for today. Faith in God recognizes that temporary injustices will fall to divine justice.

Stay wise and keep your eyes on Him. The moment that you act as if there is no God, then you are not only acting like a fool – you have become one.

CROSS EXAMINATION – *Examined by the Cross*

1. *Are there any situations in which you believe that it is necessary to act ungodly to survive?*
2. *Are there any situations in which you have to use profanity or threaten someone to be taken seriously? What happens when you act like a fool, for a foolish person to get the message?*
3. *Does it ever seem like foolish people get a free pass? Does it seem as if they get away with more?*
4. *The end result of Proverbs 29:9 indicates that there is no peace. How do you prevent irrational people from taking your peace?*

"A man groping in darkness doesn't need a lesson on darkness;
he needs light.
That light is Jesus."
Hazem Farraj

Day 14

Everyone Needs a Counselor

"Where no counsel *is*, the people fall;
but in the multitude of counsellers *there is* safety[6]."
Proverbs 11:14 KJV

Everyone in the office, except Corbin, gathered in the break room to sing *Happy Birthday* to Lydia. Annette thought it to be quite unusual for Corbin to be this antisocial.

"What's eating you?" Annette inquired as she let herself into Corbin's office. She refused to accept any answer short of a full explanation.

"It's this divorce case. My client was unemployed when we filed the case, but she has a job now. We have trial tomorrow and she's going to say that she is unemployed to get more child support," Corbin whimpered.

The ethical quandary stumped him. If he submitted a child support worksheet showing zero income, he would be lying to the court; however, if he informed the court of his client's deception, then he would be breaching attorney-client privilege. To make matters worse, he feared burning bridges with a client who was actually his neighbor.

---

[6] This is the King James Version spelling of the word "counselors."

Annette suggested that Corbin simply go forward with the lie, but to say things at trial such as "My client _says_ that she is unemployed" or "these are the figures _my client_ gave me." This way Corbin would not be lying or divulging client confidentiality. Annette also told him that this would give the judge and opposing counsel a hint that Corbin's client was not being truthful. Corbin did not like this idea. Annette's suggestion only meant deceiving the client instead of the court. As their frustrations mounted, Annette motioned through Corbin's doorway to Jason and Rebecca, two senior associates, to join their conversation.

Within moments, Jason and Rebecca developed a perfect plan. They advised Corbin to call his client on speaker phone with them in the room. Rebecca informed the client that she supervised Corbin's work and had great relations with opposing counsel and local judges in the area.

"I cannot allow a junior associate to submit perjury. Please provide us three recent paystubs or we will inform the judge that we cannot represent you and uphold our ethical obligations to the bar," Rebecca began. Within twenty minutes, the client emailed her paystubs. Rebecca and Jason easily resolved Corbin's ethical quandary.

"I can't believe you missed that good birthday cake, dealing with this simple issue. The moment you stop asking people for advice, you're no good to yourself or to anyone else. That's a dangerous place to be. Only God has all the answers. So unless you're God, you need to ask for help," Jason warned in an unusually stark tone.

Corbin had spent so much time giving counsel, he never bothered to think that he needed some too. In the multitude of counselors, there is safety.

CROSS EXAMINATION - *Examined by the Cross*

1. *Neither your education, nor your work experience will ever provide you with all of the answers. Everyone needs community and counsel daily. Read Proverbs 11:14 again. List all the people who provide you counsel? How often do you seek counsel whether from others or from God? Do you find safety from counsel?*
2. *Do you seek counsel for large and small problems or only for the large problems? Do you see a danger in only seeking counsel for major issues? Do you see the danger in not having a multitude of counselors?*
3. *Who do you counsel?*

Day 15

Tough People in Tough Times

**"If you falter in times of trouble,
how small is your strength!"
Proverbs 24:10 - NIV**

India received the phone call that changed her life. Shaking hands could not be steadied, as her father disclosed that her mother had died in her sleep during a midday nap. India's mother had been up the night before coughing and fighting fevers, but now she knew eternal peace. As India's father discussed funeral arrangements for the weekend, his calm voice finally cracked as tears fell on the other side of the phone.

India had an intense criminal trial standing between her and the funeral. In these moments, India envied her colleagues working in the larger firms who could simply give a case to another attorney in the office. The attorney loved her mother deeply; however, she realized that either the case or her grieving would have to be postponed.

India had worked too hard over the last few months to secure witnesses for her client as he sat in jail. One witness reluctantly made arrangements to take off from work to testify and would not be able to do it again if the case was postponed. Even though her mother's death crushed her heart, she had a client who needed her to win at trial. India secured the acquittal for her client, then took a flight to her hometown to assist her father and siblings.

The legal profession is a tough profession. Attorneys stress long hours over matters that have severe consequences. The work often determines the difference between a jail sentence or an acquittal and a great contract or a rotten deal. One mistake can destroy lives.

The struggle to be a Christian attorney presents additional challenges. It is often in the midst of one's own financial uncertainty that an attorney hears the cries of the poor, the oppressed, and the uninformed. It is often in the busiest times that attorneys have to respond to injustice. It is often in the midst of doing noble work where attorneys attract the ire of oppressors, exploiters, and powerful enemies.

How small is your strength? Do not let the weight of the battle, uncertainty of the times, or the size of the opposition deter you. The greater battles present more glorious victories. *How great is your strength?* You can only measure it by the size of your fight. There is a prize to be shared with God. Now is the time to embrace the fight, to refuse to falter, and to trust God for victory!

CROSS EXAMINATION – *Examined by the Cross*

1. *What is your greatest battle today?*
2. *Who is your biggest foe? Is it another person or yourself?*
3. *Have you been complacent in this battle? What is your strategy for victory?*
4. *Are you faltering? Are you feeling victorious?*

"This is the open secret of how to live as a Christian.
It is not about us struggling in vain to be more like Jesus, but allowing him, by the power of his Spirit, to come and change us from the inside.
Once again, we see that to have him as our example is not enough; we need him as our Savior."
John Stott

Day 16

The Winding Career Path

**"A man's steps are directed by the LORD,
How then can anyone understand his own way?"
Proverbs 20:24 - NIV**

"What happened to casual Friday?" asked Bernie while noticing Carly's professional attire. Carly only needed sixty copies of one sheet, yet had to wait for Bernie, the office chatterbox, to finish copying and talking.

"If you must know, I'm going to Career Day. I'll be telling high school students a bunch of lies about how the profession is so wonderful! Then, I'll get the usual questions about how much money I make and whether I like getting guilty people out of jail," Carly complained. The middle aged attorney vented to her co-worker about unfulfilled dreams of helping large groups of people. Each client brought her a different fire to put out which seemed to have nothing to do with her making the world better. The case-by-case "fire fighting" felt aimless, unrewarding, and unappreciated.

"Sometimes, I can put them out – but the majority of the time the fire started before me and will continue long after me," she concluded. Carly could not see how any pieces fitted together; moreover, she saw no greater good being accomplished from handling lawsuit after lawsuit.

"Carly, it's okay. No one truly knows their full purpose. I used to think of life like a movie and that I'd have one epic defining battle. I saw a movie about a person I admired and realized that the scriptwriter left out so many important parts of the person's life. After seeing that movie, I stopped trying to define my life in terms of epic battles anymore," offered Bernie. Suddenly, Bernie sounded less like the office clown and more like a sage as he directed Carly to view her life as God's tapestry.

He quoted elements of the Corrie ten Boom poem "Life is but a Weaving" to explain that humanity can only see the strings beneath the tapestry, but the Lord sees the woven picture from above. Bernie disagreed with the pastors and the self-help gurus who preached that there are steps to take to know one's purpose.

He argued that God may reveal some things, but man is incapable of understanding infinite wisdom, infinite purpose, and the infinite lives that are touched on a daily basis from our actions. "We get *pieces* of our purpose, but God's ways are not our ways so we can't understand *everything*. Maybe God just wants us to keep plugging away and help people along our journey," concluded Bernie.

Carly thought about the fact that God led the Israelites out of Egypt with a pillar of cloud by day and a pillar of fire by night. God did not require them to follow a plan, but His lead. Carly copied her hand-outs for the children and thanked Bernie for helping her to realize that she did not have to have all the answers. She did not have to give the children all of the keys to career satisfaction and a successful life. The children merely needed to hear the testimony of the road that she had traveled in response to God's calling.

"Trust in the LORD with all your heart and
lean not on your own understanding;
in all your ways acknowledge him and
he will make your paths straight."
Proverbs 3:5 - NIV

CROSS EXAMINATION – *Examined by the Cross*

1. *Are you disappointed about your career path?*
2. *Which of the following is true for you?*
   - ☐ I don't know if God has shown me my purpose.
   - ☐ God has not shown me my purpose
   - ☐ God has shown me my purpose, but I am not fulfilling it.
   - ☐ God has shown me my purpose and I am living it.
3. *Is it possible that the path may seem winding to you, but straight to the Lord?*
4. *Read the quote below. Does your church guide you in your purpose in life or does it simply evoke an awareness of right and wrong?*

"The Church's approach to an intelligent carpenter is usually confined to exhorting him not to be drunk and disorderly in his leisure hours, and to come to church on Sundays. What the Church should be telling him is this: that the very first demand that his religion makes upon him is that he should make good tables."
Dorothy Sayers

Day 17

FIRST FRUITS

"Honor the LORD with your wealth,
with the first fruits of all your crops;
then your barns will be filled to overflowing,
and your vats will brim over with new wine."
Proverbs 3:9-10 - NIV

Alton stared at the name on the return address on the envelope in utter puzzlement. "Cherry Plum?" chuckled the attorney as he recalled his brief foray into entertainment law. Decades ago, Alton had hopes of representing major recording artists and hearing his name announced at award shows. He heard Clara Cerise, a young waitress, singing at an open mic night and invested two years of his life helping her to record a demo and then trying to shop it to recording labels. Alton had not heard anything from Clara aka Cherry Plum in twenty-three years.

Inside the envelope, Alton found pictures of Cherry singing on stage in three different venues, a check in the amount of ten thousand dollars, and a handwritten letter. The letter narrated Cherry's ongoing pursuit of a dream. She had always promised to pay her attorney the moment she made any "real money."

Cherry signed with a major label overseas and received a signing bonus. Alton chuckled as the letter reminisced over the times that he helped lug speakers on stage for Cherry and the time that he tried to pay the pizza delivery man and got locked out of the recording studio. He had been locked out for hours because no one could hear him banging on the door.

Alton's heart burst wide open because Cherry remembered him and all that he had done for her. She shared the first fruits of her music career with him. Alton was so touched by the letter and the check that he decided to give some of it to his church and to use some of it to visit Cherry.

God's heart also opens when we return our time, talent, and treasure to Him. Genesis 4:4 states that Abel offered the fat portions of his firstborn flock and the Lord looked favorably on his sacrifices. Are you bringing the fat portions of your firstborn work? Do you give your first fruits? Are you reaping harvest after harvest in terms of your education, skills, and finances? How much of your education, skills, and finances have you devoted to the Kingdom of God and to helping His people?

Even if you are short of your goals, God has still blessed you with a harvest of knowledge, talents, and finances. He owns all of it, so please try to give some of it back to Him today.

In giving first fruits, you will experience a significant test: a test of your heart in giving to our Father in heaven and a test of your faith to let go of the things of this world to hold onto His never changing hand.

CROSS EXAMINATION – *Examined by the Cross*

1. *How would you feel if you were Alton and received a check from someone you helped? Have you adequately honored God as being the source of your success? Make an assessment of your giving (time, talent, and treasures) to the Lord and to His Kingdom.*
2. *Pray and ask God to reveal to you whether you have given sufficiently and to reveal areas in which you can give your first fruits.*

"The Living Water offered me
Was cool and quenched my thirst.
In return He wanted me
To only put Him first."
Jeanie Niemoller

Day 18

PRAISE THE DEVIL?

"Those who forsake the law praise the wicked,
but those who keep the law resist them."
Proverbs 28:4 - NIV

"So how are you doing?" inquired Yasmine to her client through the prison phone. Taylor had been in prison for three months awaiting trial since her parents lacked the means to pay bail. Taylor hesitated before answering the question. She wanted to sound confident and upbeat, but she did not want to lie and say that she was happy in prison. At times, Taylor whipped herself mentally for being "stupid" enough to try to sell drugs in the neighborhood. While at other times, Taylor hated the Kansas City Police Department for the illegal search and seizure that led to her arrest. Her brake lights worked perfectly, yet the cops pulled her over anyway.

"Yaz, I'm okay. No one is bothering me. We have bible study here, so I'm getting back into church some. It's hard to sleep some times and . . . the food. . . well, um it's garbage," Taylor laughed.

"Well, the good news is that your former Youth Pastor will be in court to speak on your behalf and your parents also spoke to two of your teachers who can testify to how well you were doing in school before you started getting into trouble," said Yasmine. Taylor's attention started to drift away in the midst of her lawyer's good news. In seconds, Taylor's countenance shifted from shame to offense.

"Yaz, I don't see the big deal or why the cops are bothering people who sell a little drugs. This is a *nonviolent* crime. I'm not shooting anyone or breaking into homes," rationalized the juvenile.

"Praise the devil! Amen!" Yasmine yelled on the phone. "You're right you have to follow the devil sometimes to make it!"

Taylor gave a nervous half laugh as she wondered if her attorney had tried to tell a joke. She did not understand where Yasmine was going with this. She always enjoyed the fact that her lawyer did not talk down to her and seemed "real," but there were also times that Yasmine became preachy.

"C'mon, let's keep it real. You know right from wrong. When you do wrong, you follow Satan and give him praise. When you do right, you follow God and give Him praise," argued Yasmine with a knock-out punch.

"I was dealing, so I guess I was praising the devil," Taylor deduced after no longer having the desire to rationalize her conduct. Even if the cops harassed her and violated her rights, she still broke the law.

"By the way, drug dealing is a *violent* crime. You poison people and communities," Yasmine corrected. She went on to explain that God will deal with the bad officers for harassing people and abusing their power. The wise attorney also raised the possibility that God may have saved her life from a bad drug deal through the bad officers. Taylor soon decided to forgive the officers, to forgive herself, and to make decisions to obey all laws and God's commands for her life. Yasmine convinced her that all grudges and unforgiveness also mount to praising the wicked. Yasmine's uncompromising outlook served as an inspiring example of a life of praise towards God.

Yasmine often took flack from Christians for representing criminals. Many from the church did not understand her ministry. The legal profession provided her direct access to people who have succumbed to evil and who may potentially falter again. Yasmine Haley refused to be the type of attorney who simply accepted money from criminals and encouraged repeat business. Yasmine refused to praise the wicked, instead she praised the word of God by living it.

CROSS EXAMINATION – *Examined by the Cross*

1. *Read Proverbs 28:4. How does bad conduct equate to praising the wicked?*
2. *How does good conduct equate to resisting the wicked?*
3. *Read the quote below. Even though Jesus is unchanging, we have an opportunity to experience Him differently based on our conduct. Based on your current circumstances, who is Jesus to you right now?*

"Jesus is all. When He judges, He is Law; when He teaches, He is Word; when He saves, He is Grace; when He begets, He is Father; when begotten He is Son; when He suffers, He is Lamb; when buried, He is Man; when risen, He is God.
Such is Jesus Christ! To Him be glory forever, amen!"
Melito, Bishop of Sardis

Day 19

SOUL WINNER

**"The fruit of the righteous is a tree of life,
and he who wins souls is wise."
Proverbs 11:30 - NIV**

Michael Vettner, Director of Human Resources for Solid Water Technologies stood in amazement of the grand affair before his eyes. Mandy Brannigan, the CEO of Solid Water, completely closed all operations to honor, Ronald Gambrills' retirement as in-house counsel. Speaker after speaker celebrated Ronald's character and integrity even more than his 35 years of service.

Mrs. Brannigan laughed as she told an anecdote from the podium about her initial meeting with Ronald when Solid Water was only a small business. She had been cheated by a major customer and even though Ronald represented the cheating customer, she felt that he had listened to her more closely than her attorney. "My attorney at the time wasn't prepared. Ronald heard my frustration and explained my demands to his client.

Ronald refused to lie for his client during the course of negotiations and encouraged him to act responsibly. He also called me out when I was unreasonable," remarked Mandy Brannigan. The CEO concluded the anecdote explaining how she tracked Ronald down and hired him as soon as the company earned enough money to afford in-house counsel.

No truer words could have been spoken of Ronald. Michael shed a few tears as he recalled the times Ronald intervened between him and a disgruntled employee. "Forgive him, Mike. He doesn't deserve it, but we didn't deserve it either," often advised Ronald. Ronald took every opportunity to invoke the gospel into casual conversations and serious meetings.

Ronald's success stood on full display. No one referred to the in-house counsel as an arm twister, shark, or hammer; in fact, each speaker described him as a gentleman who won hearts and souls. One speaker even referred to him as the "drum major for righteousness" that the Rev. Dr. Martin Luther King, Jr. preached about in a famous historical sermon. Ronald won the soul of the CEO, the company, and everyone who knew him. Michael became a better Director of Human Resources by learning from Ronald's wisdom and example as a soul winner.

CROSS EXAMINATION – *Examined by the Cross*

1. *Why does scripture indicate that there is wisdom in winning souls?*
2. *Have you won any souls?*
3. *What type of fruit have you produced?*
4. *Read the following exchange below. What does it tell you about our priorities? What does it say about our connection to Jesus Christ?*

Pope Innocent IV: You see, the day is past when the church could say, "Silver and gold have I none."

Thomas Aquinas: Yes, Holy Father. . . and the day is past when the church could say to the lame man, "Rise and walk!"

Day 20

JUSTICE FOR ALL

**"Acquitting the guilty and condemning the innocent –
the LORD detests them both."
Proverbs 17:15 - NIV**

"I guess we were foolish to think that we could trust our clerks. Someone took it upon themselves to make thousands of copies yesterday," screamed Madeline Widner, the managing partner, as she paced around the conference room table. Firm policy mandated that all employees use billing codes to track photocopies to specific clients. Madeline expressed disbelief that a law clerk would abuse firm trust.

Even with a closed conference room door, the secretaries heard Madeline's rants. After making threats to fire the next person who abuses the copier, the angry partner dismissed the law clerks to their cubicles. Madeline, then made an announcement to the secretaries and to the attorneys that she be notified the next time a clerk "steals from her firm", so she could personally "exterminate the rat."

Steven Formica, the senior partner, became puzzled as he entered the firm reception area. Everyone seemed to be on edge. Steven quietly called Ava, his secretary, to his office.

"All I know is that Madeline came into the office yesterday and found hundreds of copies of a flier on the copier and went off," said Ava. Ava, then repeated the managing partner's threat to fire anyone caught making copies.

"I'm disappointed to hear that, especially since I was with Madeleine in the office last night when we caught Courtney making the copies. I can't believe she basically let Courtney off the hook and then shamed the other clerks," Steven confided. He was disgusted that the managing partner had shamed innocent law clerks while acquitting the actual culprit. By keeping the clerks in a pointless sixty minute meeting, they had to work an extra hour to meet their billables. "I may have to re-think this partnership. This is not only cowardly, this is an injustice," finished Steven.

Even as a criminal defense attorney, Steven would not attempt to acquit the guilty. Instead, he encouraged clients to accept responsibility then negotiated a fair plea agreement.

As a proponent of justice, Steven also fought prosecutors tooth and nail to prevent the conviction of the innocent. Steven could not allow this injustice to continue in his firm. He found it disgraceful to reprimand innocent law clerks and to take them away from their work.

The next morning, Steven apologized to the clerks in front of the firm for their undeserved humiliation. The senior partner, then announced the firing of Madeline and her niece, Courtney.

"Niece? That explains a lot!" Ava giggled until catching Steven's disapproving glare. Steven explained that God hates double standards and how injustice opposes His nature and His character.

CROSS EXAMINATION – *Examined by the Cross*

1. *Have you ever been in a situation in which, you felt that you were being punished or reprimanded for someone else's actions?*
2. *Do you see Madeline's handling of the clerks as an injustice or do you believe that this is an acceptable way to discreetly send a message to the entire group without naming the guilty party?*
3. *Does injustice discourage you or motivate you?*
4. *Did injustice discourage or motivate Steven to action?*

"Disappointments are inevitable,
but discouragement is a choice."
Charles Stanley

Day 21

The Chocolate Stronghold

**"Like a city whose walls are broken down
is a man who lacks self-control."
Proverbs 25:28 - NIV**

"Get out of my office!" screamed Felix at Gwen, the new temp. The staff had a good laugh at Felix's feigned rage. Gwen misunderstood the joke. She puzzled over how she invoked his wrath simply by trying to sell Girl Scout Cookies for her daughter's troop. Gwen mistakenly concluded that she must have been deemed unprofessional for selling cookies in a firm setting.

"Gwen, it's okay. Felix is a self-professed recovering chocoholic. He has diabetes and high cholesterol," explained Ronin from IT.

"Felix used to bring in donuts, cookies, cupcakes, . . .you name it. . . to the office. . . on special occasions. . .random days, you name it," added Tina.

"You could always go to his office and get a few small chocolate candy bars from his candy dish," said Ronin.

"Those were the good ol' days!"remarked Wyatt as he suddenly blushed with guilt from his co-workers' disapproving looks. "I'm sorry he has diabetes and heart problems, I just missed. . . the candy. . . never mind."

Gwen listened to a saddening tale of a successful attorney who suffered two heart attacks before reaching his 45th birthday. Felix Grubauer, an Iraq War veteran, served active duty, yet almost died due to the inability to control his cravings. Felix and his wife, Arlene, held equal culpability for his poor health. Even after the first heart attack, Arlene made it clear that she had no desire of changing her eating habits. She laughed when her husband brought healthy snacks to the house and filled the pantry with even more deserts.

Despite his high level of education, wealth, and professional accomplishments, Felix had a weakness. The second heart attack finally convinced Arlene to listen to Felix's pleas for help. Felix realized that he was weak, vulnerable, and a dead man if he could not find self-control. Felix once joked with Arlene in the hospital that they wasted money on the home security system when chocolate chip cookies posed his greatest threat.

Arlene later met with the office staff to request that everyone help Felix where he was vulnerable. The couple vowed to take a radical approach to defeat the addiction that had been defeating Felix's health and happiness.

"Girl Scout cookies! Get behind me, Satan!" yelled Felix from his office for one last laugh.

Proverbs 25:28 compares a man without self-control to a city with broken walls. Addiction, fits of anger, procrastination, pornography, lust, excessive criticism, verbal abuse, dissension, lying, excessive eating or dieting, and idolatry are examples of areas where people lack self control. These are areas in which many have broken walls; however, walls can be repaired.

CROSS EXAMINATION – *Examined by the Cross*

1. *Re-read Proverbs 25:28.*
2. *What are the breached walls in your life? What are the areas in which you lack self control? What are you doing to gain control?*
3. *Have you confessed your strongholds to God and trusted loved ones? Do you feel as vulnerable as a city with no walls? Have you helped others to strengthen their self control? Are you sympathetic?*

Day 22

Preceded Reputation

**"Even a child is known by his actions,
by whether his conduct is pure and right."
Proverbs 20:11 - NIV**

"Sam, how are the little ones? I'm guessing Kevin and Kena are about nine and seven by now," said Robert Channing to Samuel Pyle, Judge Palmerro's clerk, in the court hallway. Due to the sensitive matter of the cases, the city court house required parties and their attorneys to wait for trial in the hallway. Robert and his client, Danny Lucerna, extended smug smiles to their adversaries. They gloated over Robert's familiarity with the court house and court staff. Denise tried to push down the lump in her throat as Sam approached her. She had already disclosed to her client that this was her first trial in the city, so Robert Channing's grandstanding only made the experience more intimidating.

"How long do you expect your trial to last?" Sam asked Denise.

"We have three witnesses, so I anticipate at least a three hour hearing," offered Denise.

"I noticed in your complaint that you only asked for two thousand dollars in legal fees and included copies of the checks that you received. That was pretty cool. We don't see that much. Honesty. . . I mean – we don't see honesty much. Most lawyers ask for amounts that they never earned. Don't tell anyone, but the judge and the law clerk who saw your pleadings were impressed. You seem like an honest person," said Sam.

His words calmed Denise's insecurities. As Sam started to walk back into the courtroom, Denise darted to him to tap his shoulders.

"You only asked *me* for an estimate of the trial length. Why didn't you ask Robert Channing? Did you two have a conversation already?" asked Denise suspicious of court misconduct and favoritism with the lawyer who knew Sam on a first name basis.

"Everyone in the courthouse knows Mr. Channing quite well. He lies all the time. He'll give an hour estimate just to have his case called first. After we call his case, then he'll pull out a lot of exhibits and call several witnesses. The judges can't stand him," Sam explained.

Denise now realized the truth in the words that her father told her as a child. People are always watching, so it is important to be honest and to walk in integrity. She had a reputation for honesty even before stepping into the courtroom. Robert Channing's reputation for dishonesty preceded him. Integrity is our allegiance towards God. Integrity is our witness towards man.

> "A good name is to more desirable
> than great riches.
> to be esteemed is better than silver or gold."
> **Proverbs 22:1 - NIV**

CROSS EXAMINATION – *Examined by the Cross*

1. *Have you ever been in a situation in which your reputation preceded you? Were you pleasantly surprised or disappointed?*
2. *In the legal profession, some people take pride in having a reputation for being aggressive, mean, and abrupt. How do you deal with being seen as rational or a peacemaker with people who do not value those characteristics?*
3. *There is value in having a good reputation and a good name, but even Jesus was considered a criminal, a blasphemer, and a lunatic. How do you know when to consider what people think about you verses when to ignore your reputation?*

Day 23

WHITE KNIGHT

**"Do not exploit the poor because they are poor
and do not crush the needy in court."
Proverbs 22:22 - NIV**

The junior partner handed Lauren Conrad a Finelli Holdings case file with a stern *"don't lose this case, this is a good client"* look. Lauren excitedly dove into the documents only to find that Finelli intended to take the home of Cheyenne Gloce, a sympathetically foolish widow. Mr. Gloce's death left her in a financial bind that led her to fall behind on property taxes. Cheyenne held over two hundred eighty thousand dollars in equity, but no liquid cash to pay a three thousand dollar tax debt. By county law, the house had to be sold to pay the unpaid property taxes.

Unfortunately, Cheyenne relied on Finelli's white knight ads and the company promise to help people to avoid losing their lifelong dream. Finelli lent her three thousand dollars conditioned on a full repayment within three months plus a thousand dollars in interest and fees. Failure to pay would result in the lost of the home and all of the equity in the property.

Her payment history to Finelli Holdings showed a reasonable attempt to make payments toward the loan, but Cheyenne could not pay the principal and high interest rate within the short three month window. This failure gave Finelli the legal right to foreclose on the home that she owned for over thirty-two years. Lauren reasoned that the widow would have been better off selling the home and keeping the profit or refinancing it to pay off the tax debt. The white knight loan was a scam.

Lauren's conscience could not handle the enormity of Cheyenne's foolishness and Finelli's predatory ways. Finelli's three thousand dollar loan would net them two hundred and seventy-seven thousand dollars of equity that the Gloces held in the property. They were clearly taking advantage of someone who was less educated and grieving a death. Even after Cheyenne attempted to pay the full balance of the loan, Finelli refused to accept any payment after the loan repayment period ended and opted to foreclose on the property.

Lauren violated firm policy by calling Mr. Finelli and trying to convince him to give Cheyenne a break. Her client repeatedly explained that the parties had a deal that had been breached. Despite their advertisements, Finelli Holdings made most of their profits by taking homes instead of saving them.

Realizing that she had an ethical duty to represent an unethical client, Lauren joked, "I will represent you in court but on Judgment Day, you're on your own."

Lauren was just as shocked by her comment as Mr. Finelli. The partners could fire her for misconduct in offending a "good" client. They could also terminate her for hurting firm profits by telling a client to drop a lawsuit. Silence weighed on attorney and client for several intense seconds until Mr. Finelli found a response.

"I won't be needing you to represent me in court or on Judgment Day, Ms. Conrad. I've been thinking about getting out of the business for awhile now. Tell Cheyenne Gloce that we'll release the note," Finelli ordered.

The partners in the firm would later mockingly call their associate "Saint Lauren" for having a "bleeding heart" for the poor, but she honored God by her refusal to exploit the less fortunate. Over the next few years, Lauren realized that she was not enough light to overcome the darkness of the firm and firm clients, so she resigned to work for a legal aid clinic.

CROSS EXAMINATION – *Examined by the Cross*

1. *Lauren boldly brought her faith into her workplace. Have you crossed the line between office professionalism and your faith? How did you feel? What was the response?*
2. *Lauren convinced Finelli Holding to void a legally enforceable contract out of guilt of exploiting the poor. If Finelli offered loans to people in dire need, why would Lauren accuse them of exploiting the poor?*
3. *Have you taken any action to protect the poor? Have you taken any action that exploited the poor, the uneducated, or the vulnerable?*

CHAPTER 3

TRIALS OF THE SEASONS

"Sow your seed in the morning,
and at evening let not your hand be idle,
for you do not know which will succeed,
whether this or that,
or whether both will do equally well."
Ecclesiastes 11:6 NIV

Day 24

TURN, TURN, TURN

**"There is a time for everything,
and a season for every activity under heaven."
Ecclesiastes 3:1 - NIV**

"If I didn't know any better, I'd think the judge was flirting with you," Dalton suggested as Sheila Kent gathered her exhibits.

"Judge Avery wasn't flirting, but we definitely have a history," Sheila smirked.

"Do tell," Dalton pressed his attorney for details.

"Not that kind of history. We battled in several cases. He had no respect for me as a professional, and cut me off whenever I spoke. I don't know if it was because I'm a woman, if it was because I quoted scripture in some of my opening arguments, or both, but he was quite rude to me," Sheila recounted. In her first case before Judge Avery, he interrupted her opening statement and informed her that she should save the sermons for church.

In her second appearance before Judge Avery, he rudely cut her off five minutes into the cross-examination of a witness. Avery yelled at her to move things along even though the other attorney had the witness on the stand for hours.

"Everything changed during the Dalgett case. Judge Avery yelled at my client to provide a 'yes' or 'no' answer to a question, but my client wanted to explain the answer. Avery threatened to hold my client in contempt of court unless he answered 'yes' or 'no'. I lost it. I told him that my client's right to due process permits him the right to give a full answer to any question and he can't answer a loaded question 'yes' or 'no'," Sheila narrated.

"So what did he say?" asked Dalton as the two exited the courtroom and entered the corridor.

"He yelled at me. He told me that anyone with half a brain can give a 'yes' or 'no' answer to a 'yes' or 'no' question and that he would hold my client and me in contempt of court if my client refused to do so," Sheila said with a smirk.

"So I asked him if he enjoys committing acts of terrorism – yes or no," Sheila laughed. Judge Avery's anger only escalated after being upstaged and embarrassed by Sheila. He, then, ordered the bailiff to hold Sheila and her client in contempt of court. Not backing down, Sheila informed him that she would file a complaint with the judicial disabilities commission for his abuse of authority. She further quoted scriptures and reminded him that he would answer to God for every abuse of power and that he would answer to the people who trusted him to be fair and forthright.

"I wish I had known this before my hearing," Dalton remarked.

"Everything is fine. He didn't hold us in contempt. I've been before him several times since then. He now respects me as a woman, as a lawyer, and as a Christian. God has softened his heart, so we don't have those battles anymore," Sheila concluded.

As Sheila's seasons had changed, Judge Avery's seasons also changed. She experienced a season of meekness, a season of confrontation, and now a season of comradery. Judge Avery experienced a season of arrogance, a season of humility, and now a season of comradery. For everything there is a season. Enemies and battles only endure for a season.

CROSS EXAMINATION – *Examined by the Cross*

1. *Have you ever encountered a person who was an enemy for a season?*
2. *What circumstances changed so that you no longer had to battle this individual?*
3. *Through that battle, did God change that person, you, the circumstances, or all of the above?*
4. *What wisdom have you imparted upon your enemies?*
5. *What wisdom have you obtained from your battles?*
6. *Do you avoid confrontations?*

"But if the church will free itself from the shackles of a deadening status quo and recovering its great historic mission, will speak and act fearlessly and insistently in terms of justice and peace, it will enkindle the imagination of mankind and fire the souls of men, imbuing them with a glowing and ardent love for truth, justice and peace."
Rev. Dr. Martin Luther King, Jr.

Day 25

Birthed Through Death

"There is a time for everything,
and a season for every activity under heaven:
a time to be born and a time to die."
Ecclesiastes 3:1-2 NIV (in part)

Deangelo's heart raced as he checked his text messages under the conference table. It had vibrated twice before in the morning meeting; however, this message said, "Papi, the baby is coming.[7]" As he scooped up his papers, everyone clapped and cheered for the expectant first time father. Deangelo received a few pats on the back as he left the conference room. One of the partners insisted that a co-worker drive him.

"Great, now we'll lose even more billable hours with two attorneys out of the office," Alistaire the managing partner joked.

Nick Collinsworth convinced Deangelo with the winning argument that he could get to the baby faster if he were dropped off and didn't have to park. Within minutes, Nick dropped his colleague off in front of the hospital doors.

---

[7] Papi is Spanish for "daddy" or "father."

Deangelo quickly ascended the hospital elevator to the 5th floor. His mother-in-law's half-hearted greeting confirmed every fear that something could go or had gone wrong. Mrs. Chengzhu's face signaled that Deangelo's wife, baby, or both were in grave danger. Something had to be wrong if Mrs. Chengzhu stood in a waiting room instead of being with his wife. Something was definitely wrong for her to greet him in any manner except with a big hug and cheek kiss.

A surgeon, a grief counselor, and a few other members of the hospital staff soon flanked Deangelo and Mrs. Chengzhu with good news of a healthy 6 pound 6 ounce baby girl and terrible news of the life that passed in transporting baby Gabriela into this world.

Deangelo had never cried so hard in his life. He praised God for the indescribable miracle of birth while grieving over the incredible toll that this miracle took on his wife.

Throughout the pain over the next five to ten years, Deangelo professed his indomitable faith often quoting Job in saying, "Shall I accept only the good from God." He advised friends and family to never take life for granted. Every birthday party that his daughter enjoyed also marked the anniversary of his wife's death.

In Deangelo's loss and heaven's gain, he became a more balanced and focused father. In his season of joy and suffering, he felt the comforting unchanging hand of the Lord and the blessed assurance of the continuity of life in this world into the next. As a born again Christian, he too experienced birth through death: life through the crucifixion and life through death to self.

CROSS EXAMINATION – *Examined by the Cross*

1. *What thoughts or reflections, if any, come about when you hear of a birth of a child?*
2. *What thoughts or reflections, if any, come about when you hear of a death of a person?*
3. *Just like baby Gabriela, we have been birthed through death. Jesus Christ paid the ultimate cost for us to experience life and life more abundantly. There is a time to be born and a time to die. Never take life for granted. Be ever willing to live for Him and to die for Him in every season.*

Day 26

GREEN THUMB TYCOON

"A time to plant and a time to uproot."
Ecclesiastes 3:2 NIV (in part)

"So often people ask me the secrets of great investing and how I managed to make so much money from my business ventures. The truth of the matter, fifty percent of my success came from making good investments and fifty percent of my success came from withdrawing from my bad investments," shared Shirley Ripka from a panel of entrepreneurial giants.

Shirley graduated from law school while working as an investment banker. Instead of going the traditional law firm route, Shirley used her legal background to transform her limited liability company into a publicly traded corporation.

Shirley credited Mark 11:12-25 for changing her perspective of Jesus Christ and the gospel. "I had always thought of Jesus as a passive, all accepting, laid back, hippie of a Savior before I read these verses. Jesus cursed a fig tree because it was unproductive," said the investment guru.

Productive people know that their calling to bear fruit in this world requires them to spend a considerable amount of time sowing seeds and uprooting unfruitful ventures.

Shirley preached, "There are people in whom you should *invest* your time. There are people whom you should *stop investing* time. There are activities in which you should *invest* your time and there are some from which you need to *divest*. There is information which you should expose yourself to and there are resources and media which you need to uproot from your mind and spirit."

Some of the members of the audience reflected upon their work effort and whether they had been too lazy to sow seeds into their future. While others reflected upon their passivity and whether they had been too tolerant with spiritual and financial weeds.

CROSS EXAMINATION – *Examined by the Cross*

1. *Identify five areas in your life where you need to start sowing.*
2. *Identify five areas in your life which need to be uprooted.*

Day 27

WHEN CHRISTIANS KILL AND HEAL

"A time to kill and a time to heal."
Ecclesiastes 3:3 NIV (in part)

Three attorneys and four secretaries in the firm openly professed their faith and met for bible study on Wednesdays during lunch. Two of the attorneys, Claudette and Wilma, intrigued the group partially because they were twin sisters and partially because of their diverse experiences.

During one lunch break bible study, Claudette and Wilma laughed at how they could not have been more different, yet still held a love for the gospel of Christ. Prior to law school, Claudette spent two tours in Iraq on active duty. She came from a military family which preached that there was no greater honor than serving the country. Claudette shared with her co-workers one occasion in which she had to shoot a person who intended to harm a friend. The would-be assailant had no affiliation with any army, but simply attempted to rob and kill a friend while they were off base, on leave.

Wilma shared her testimony of missionary efforts taken after college to bring medical supplies to war torn villages in Sudan. Her church organized a group to share the light of Christ to those in the shadows of genocide. Wilma recalled one occasion in which she saved the life of an eleven year old by applying a tourniquet. Even though Wilma broke away from her family tradition of military service, she still found a way to be a soldier for the Lord. Despite Wilma's soft spoken tone and Claudette's brash, in-your-face directness, the two testified to their battles in various hot spots throughout the world.

Throughout the Bible, the Lord called great leaders of the faith such as Moses, King David, and Deborah to *kill* enemies of the kingdom. Throughout the Bible, the Lord called great leaders of the faith such as Elijah, Peter, and Paul to *heal* for the glory of the kingdom. There is an equal amount of love and obedience required in both acts.

CROSS EXAMINATION – *Examined by the Cross*

1. *If God ever calls you to kill or to heal, how would you respond to such a calling?*
2. *Have you ever done either?*
3. *Do you agree with the statement that "there is an equal amount of love and obedience required in both acts"? Wouldn't that depend on your disposition?*

Day 28

BREAK TO BUILD

"A time to tear down and a time to build."
Ecclesiastes 3:3 NIV (in part)

Gary patted the breast pocket of his Oxford blue dress shirt for a pack of cigarettes. He had been tobacco free for eighteen months, but this was the first time that he had hated himself for quitting. Gary always relied on his partners, Oscar and Scarlett, to make the tough personnel decisions.

"C'mon, Gary. It's time to man up! Oscar did us dirty. He took some of our biggest clients and took two of our best rainmakers in Chesimard and Igbhi. We need to bring in some real power players if we're going to keep the firm going. That means we have to cut some dead weight too. I like Monty, but we can't sustain him," Scarlett argued.

Monty Tasco mentored Gary and Scarlett when they were young associates, so when they started Shezinsky, Michaels, and Slayton they hired their mentor. Monty was their first employee and a delightful presence in the office.

The partners had initially hoped that Monty would bring in enough business and become a partner within a few years; however, Monty appeared to prefer being fed cases as opposed to bringing in new clients. Gary feared the backlash from the remaining associates and staff. He knew that everyone would worry about their jobs if they could be ruthless enough to fire a mainstay like Monty.

"Let people get mad. Some people will trust our vision. We need a meritocracy. The people who stay on board are the ones who contribute to the growth of the firm. Monty isn't doing it. He isn't a *rainmaker*, he's a *drizzle maker*. He barely does enough to cover what we pay him," concluded Scarlet. Gary did not sleep well that night. In the wee hours of the morning, he emailed his consent to fire Monty to his partners. Scarlet had been awake too and emailed him a thank you for agreeing to make the tough decision.

As anticipated, Monty's termination created some tension within the firm. They lost a few attorneys and a few members of the staff who questioned whether the partners would be loyal to anyone if they could fire a stalwart like Monty. Despite the initial bumps, the firm reached unprecedented prosperity over the next five years.

The Bible provides a poignant example of having to break in order to build. After seventy years of Babylonian captivity, the Israelite exiles returned to their homeland to rebuild the altar, to rebuild the temple, and to rebuild the wall that protected the city. Imagine their sunken hearts as they saw their altar and temple in ruins. More than cultural significance, the altar and the temple represented the presence and favor of God.

In order to *build*, the children of God would have to *tear* down fear and doubt, *tear* down pride and the petty divisions within, *tear* down complacency, and, if necessary, *tear* down any opposition. The Israelites often had to *build* walls while carrying weapons in one hand. Imagine needing one hand to build and another hand for defense.

Priest Ezra and Governor Nehemiah sought the rebuilding of the altar, the temple, and the city wall in the face of opposition from within their community and from groups outside of their community.

"But many of the older priests and Levites and family heads, who had seen the former temple, wept aloud when they saw the foundation of this temple being laid, while many others shouted for joy. No one could distinguish the sound of the shouts of joy from the sound of weeping, because the people made so much noise. And the sound was heard from far away."
Ezra 3:12-13 - NIV

The older saints and leaders mourned progress out of fear of tearing away from the past. Seasons of growth often produce joy and weeping.

CROSS EXAMINATION – *Examined by the Cross*

1. *What has God called you to tear down?*
2. *What has God called you to build?*
3. *Who will celebrate your efforts?*
4. *Who will mourn your efforts?*
5. *Who is your opposition? Have you ever felt as if you were building with one hand and needing another hand for defense?*
6. *What steps do you take to ensure that you are improving and not simply doing the same things?*

"Rebounding should never mean forcing up another bad shot.
It should mean creating the opportunity
for a new and improved shot."
Vera Jones

Day 29

CAUGHT ON CAMERA

"A time to weep and a time to laugh."
Ecclesiastes 3:4 NIV (in part)

Former Mayor Phaedra Wilmott's funeral shut down the entire city. Many traveled from all over the nation to pay final respect to the renowned public servant, while others sought a significant networking opportunity with notable leaders in government and industry.

Unlike many of the vultures that descended upon the memorial service, Denny Hillendale, senior partner of The Hillendale Firm, actually knew Mayor Wilmott quite well. Even prior to her first term in office, he vigorously supported her campaign with financial contributions and even hosted fundraisers. Denny enjoyed some of the eulogies and speeches of the funeral guests who eloquently captured the mayor's achievements and personality, but deplored other speeches that were mired in partisan rhetoric and opportunistic political plugs.

Denny had been put off by the news crews and photographers that lined the corridors of the massive cathedral. "There's no respect. Funerals are no place for a media circus," Denny thought.

Periodically, Denny lost control of his emotions and wept in front of his partners and staff. He could not help but to think about the good times he had with his friend. Denny remembered one campaign incident in which reporters filmed Phaedra kissing a baby. The tape on the diaper loosened as the child unloaded. The baby kissing moment quickly became a nightmare as the four month old soiled the mayoral candidate's blouse. Without missing a beat, Phaedra changed the baby on national television. As she employed baby wipes, she promised to be just as thorough in cleaning up her city.

Denny reminded his partner, Lydia, of this incident and the two laughed hysterically. News cameras caught the two laughing during the funeral. People seated in the rows behind Denny and Lydia openly conveyed their disapproval of the two for their seemingly inappropriate and insensitive laughter.

Lydia whispered another humorous anecdote into Denny's ear which caused laughter that could not be stifled either. The two tried to be sensitive to their surroundings and tried to appear solemn, but the cameras had already caught their revelry.

After another half hour of intermittent speeches and hymns, Denny stood at the podium with a crumpled speech in his right hand. In his heart, Denny believed that the mourners had plenty of time to weep. In his heart, he opined that any true memorial to Phaedra Wilmott would be a farce if it lacked humor.

The senior partner of The Hillendale Firm took the funeral attendees through five minutes of hilarious accounts of Mayor Phaedra Wilmott's and citizen Phaedra Wilmott's greatest and most embarrassing moments. The Wilmott family later thanked Denny for the joy that he brought in the midst of their sorrow. They had forgotten about the diaper incident and laughed about it for a long time even while on camera. The funeral now reflected the family's season of weeping and laughter that they had experienced over the last few days in remembrance of Phaedra Wilmott.

The pastor chuckled as he reclaimed the podium and left the congregation with a benediction and final thought. Pastor Lawton said, "Proverbs 17:22 reminds us that a joyful heart is good medicine, but a crushed spirit dries up the bones. We will always remember the medicine that the mayor gave us through laughter."

CROSS EXAMINATION – *Examined by the Cross*

1. *Christians must understand that it is okay to laugh and to mourn depending on the season. If the Lord laughs (Psalm 2:4) and weeps (John 11:35), then it must be okay for us to do so as well.*
2. *Have you ever laughed at a time when no one else was laughing? Was your laughing appropriate?*
3. *Have you ever cried at a time when no one else was crying? Was your crying appropriate?*
4. *How do you determine when someone's season of grieving is appropriate? How do you determine what is a healthy or unhealthy amount of grieving?*

Day 30

MOURNING TO DANCING

"A time to mourn and a time to dance."
Ecclesiastes 3:4 NIV (in part)

"Judgment in favor of Plaintiff," pronounced Judge Spencer. Kamar Feders, Plaintiff's counsel, gently pushed his chair away from the desk, stood up, and hugged his client, Natalie Krausse-Vanacek. Although Natalie felt relieved to retain custody of the children, relieved to be awarded child support and alimony, and relieved that the judge did not believe the multitude of lies that her now ex-husband, Travis, had told in court, she expressed no joy, even as her sister and parents embraced her.

"Perhaps, you missed it. . . Nat, your lawyer won," consoled, Evgeny Krausse, Natalie's father, to lighten the moment.

"I'm so happy for you," screeched Natalie's younger sister Patty. For over a decade, Patty observed Natalie's inexorable suffering through a tumultuous marriage. The twelve months of marital separation marked a period in which Patty finally began to see glimmers of the sister that she knew and loved.

"It's okay, everyone. This is how people should act after a divorce. There is no winning. This can be a time to mourn – rejoicing may come later," Kamar said as he led his client and her family out of the courtroom and into the hallway. He reasoned that a period of mourning provides a healthy time of reflection. Mourning offers an opportunity to draw closer to God, an opportunity to prioritize life activities, and an opportunity to appreciate good times in the past.

Kamar grabbed Natalie's hand and reached towards Patty's hand. Patty thought it unusual for an attorney to invite her and her family to pray, but completed the circle anyway. Tears rolled down Natalie's eyes as she mourned the death of a marriage. Two had cleaved into one only to be torn apart into two again. A covenant had been broken. Natalie cried about the great times in the marriage that will never be relived, cried about the bad times in the marriage that hurt her, and cried about the marriage that could have been except for Mr. Vanacek's violent temperament.

Kamar concluded his prayer with a petition to God for: deliverance for Mr. Vanacek from his anger; deliverance for Natalie from hurt, disappointment, and shame; and deliverance for the children from any feeling of brokenness in now having a broken home. The counselor shared a verse from the book of Malachi.

Malachi 2:16 sets forth: **"I hate divorce," says the Lord God of Israel, "and I hate a man's covering himself with violence as well as his garment," says the Lord Almighty. So guard yourself in your spirit and do not break faith."** Kamar asked everyone to continue praying for Mr. Vanacek's peace. It was one thing to divorce your spouse, but another level of being lost to be divorced from God.

In Matthew 5:5, Jesus professes that mourners are blessed for they shall be comforted. Godly sorrow puts people into a position to feel God's heart for the world and to see their responsibility to touch the world.

Years after the divorce, Natalie *danced* with all of her might at her wedding reception when she remarried a born again, anger-free, Travis Vanacek. Some thought it strange for Natalie's divorce attorney to be an invited guest, but the bride and groom viewed him as a witness of God's redemptive ability to separate every sin as far as the east is from the west. On the night of the wedding, Kamar whispered into Natalie's ear, "There's a time to mourn and a time to dance, but I thank God that He's been there with you through them both."

CROSS EXAMINATION – *Examined by the Cross*

1. Was there ever a time in your life that your mourning turned into dancing?
2. Was there ever a season in your life in which you celebrated something that should have been mourned or mourned something that should have been celebrated?
3. When was the last time you mourned to the point of crying tears? When was the last time you rejoiced to the point of dancing?
4. How does repentance span mourning and celebration?

"There is a holiness about your tears.
Each one is a prayer that only God can understand.
He created them and shed them Himself.
They are His reminder to you that your soul can have
no rainbows,
if your eyes can have no tears."
Kathe Wunnenberg

Day 31

GATHERING MEANING

**"A time to scatter stones and
a time to gather them."
Ecclesiastes 3:5 - NIV (in part)**

Tab could not help but to laugh at himself for being stumped. The drive home provided him ample time to try to figure out the answer, but the time only produced more questions. The criminal defense attorney enjoyed the perspective that inmates shared during one-on-one time in the prison ministry. Hugo, a convicted jewel thief, had him perplexed as they discussed the meaning of Ecclesiastes 3:5. Hugo related to the scripture stating that at times he had to "scatter" and "fence" stolen stones and then there were times he profited by "gathering" and stealing the stones. Hugo knew the Bible would not advocate criminal activity and asked for a better interpretation of why gathering and scattering stones were good things in different seasons.

Tab attempted to explain that the scripture did not apply to illegal activity. "I guess it's saying that there are times we collect things and times that we have to give up things," Tab offered.

He had earned the nickname, "Tab" because he gave freely and graciously often telling people not to worry about repaying him. He joked that he would just put it on their tab, yet never did.

"But verse 6 already says that there's a time to keep and a time to throw away, so this verse has to mean something different, right?" asked Hugo.

Tab decided that he would call his pastor to find out the historical significance of scattering and gathering stones. He wondered if this referred to Jewish customs of building shrines and altars. *"Perhaps King Solomon, in his wisdom, suggested that there are seasons to build altars and seasons to tear down altars,"* Tab thought. As a Christian attorney, Tab knew that he built an altar for God, but pondered whether he may have unknowingly built altars to idols that needed to be scattered.

The Jewish people also used stones to delineate boundaries and property lines. *"Maybe Solomon stated that there are seasons for tearing down and creating new boundaries,"* Tab hypothesized with equal conviction.

Tab also deduced that the scripture could refer to seasons of play and seasons of work. There is a time to scatter stones by skipping them across a river and a time to gather stones to build a structure. Tab struggled with having a good balance of work and play, so perhaps he needed to scatter more rocks.

At times, his hyper-analytical mind overwhelmed him. All he needed was a simple answer to Hugo's question. After speaking to his pastor, Tab returned to the prison to share with Hugo that he did not understand the scripture and to pray to God for personalized understanding.

CROSS EXAMINATION - *Examined by the Cross*

1. *Have you ever gathered stones and cast them? How so?*
2. *What does this scripture mean to you?*
3. *How do you differentiate this scripture from Ecclesiastes 3:6?*

Day 32

The Anointed "No"

"A time to embrace and a time to refrain."
Ecclesiastes 3:5 NIV (in part)

"Stop trying to be everyone's 911!" Cameron advised. Tierra despised venturing into this terrain with her husband. He could not understand the pressures of being the only attorney in the family. She wanted him to accept the fact that the heightened responsibility came with the territory. The Bible makes it clear that "to whom much is given, much is required" and Tierra believed that she had been given much. God blessed her with a legal mind and a legal education, so she had to bear the cross, toughen up, and help people when they needed it. This meant that there would be some inconveniences.

"God didn't call you to run around like a headless chicken. Sometimes you have to prioritize and give the anointed 'no'," added Cameron.

"What is the anointed 'no'?" Tierra inquired.

"Just as God calls us and anoints us to carry a cross, He also calls us away from things. I'm not saying that things are beneath us, but we are anointed to do other things," Cameron explained. With years of experience in being married to an attorney, Cameron learned to support his arguments with examples and authorities.

"Martha attempted to serve Jesus with exuberance, but Jesus told her that her sister Mary chose the better thing by standing still at His side. Jesus *didn't call them* to serve Him in that moment. Jethro told his son-in-law, Moses, to delegate authority. Moses *wasn't called* to judge every single dispute. Jesus *refused to* perform miracles before Herod and unbelievers. . . should I go on? You don't always have to jump up and do things to prove that you are a Christian or out of guilt that people will think you're stuck up," Cameron argued triumphantly as his wife allowed the phone call from her sister to go to voicemail.

Tierra had talked to her sister for over an hour a day for the last five days about minor office disputes. Tierra admitted that she needed rest and did not have the time to get involved in another one of her sister's manufactured crises.

Cameron showed her a verse from the Bible:

**"Simply let your 'Yes' be 'Yes,' and your 'No,' 'No';
anything beyond this comes from the evil one."
Matthew 5:37 - NIV**

He explained that the verse wasn't only about keeping promises, but Jesus also suggests that it is okay to tell someone 'no'. Tierra had never read the scripture in this context before.

There is a time for us to embrace service and a time to refrain from service. There is a time for us to embrace a person, a church, or an organization, and a time to refrain from a person, a church, or an organization. As God has anointed you to say, "Yes" to certain assignments, He has also anointed you to say, "No" to other tasks.

CROSS EXAMINATION – *Examined by the Cross*

1. *Are you trying to be everyone's 911?*
2. *Are you trying to be a Messiah instead of leading them to the Savior?*
3. *Are you too busy serving the Lord to hear from the Lord?*
4. *Do you need to practice giving the anointed "No"?*
5. *Please read Luke 10:38-42. Are you more like Mary or Martha?*

Day 33

Case Law

"A time to search and a time to give up."
Ecclesiastes 3:6 NIV (in part)

In one split second, Raymond slapped his laptop off the desk onto the floor in his home office. He could hear his wife rising from their bed and leaving their bedroom. Although he was frustrated and upset, he had no intention of awaking his wife.

"Raymond, it's time to let it go. You had a trial – they found him guilty, you filed an appeal– it was denied, you asked the governor for a pardon – they denied clemency, you filed a writ of *habeas* thing to go to federal court – they rejected that too, it is what it is," consoled Natasha.[8]

"It is what it is! So that's what I'm going to say to Elan's family after he's executed," Raymond screamed as he scanned case after case for appealable grounds.

"How can you be 100% certain that he didn't do it? Didn't he confess to the murder?" Natasha inquired.

---

[8] In capital murder cases, an attorney may file a writ of *habeas corpus* after losing an appeal to cite constitutional violations in the conviction of the defendant.

"He confessed after being handcuffed to a chair for nine hours and beatened! I'd confess to anything at that point," Raymond corrected. The attorney's entire body was sore, especially his neck. It was 3:41 in the morning. Raymond had worked on the Elan Weigend case for four straight years without pay while only earning moderate revenue from other clients.

Natasha's income supported the household expenses and even carried the firm at times. His obsession with the case had no limit. Raymond even tried to work with the Weigend family to start an unsuccessful PR campaign.

Natasha looked at the piles of paper that had fallen from the printer onto the floor. The "change toner" message flashed on the printer. Raymond had used up the black toner and the cyan toner printing out cases.

"God, called you to be Elan's attorney. God never said that you'd win. You've been there for the family. You listened to him. You showed the police department and even the State the holes in the system. Please get some sleep, so you'll be rested when you see him. Show him the love of Christ one more time on this side of heaven, before he goes on to see the Savior on the other side," Natasha concluded as if making a closing argument.

"Sustained. I'm not doing anyone any good tonight. I'm not going to find any case law that'll change anything," Raymond acknowledged in the midst of his frustration.

"I'm getting better at knowing when to try to debate my lawyer husband and when to give up. There's a blessing in knowing what to do in each season," Natasha ended with an extended hand as she led her husband to their bedroom.

Christians must wisely discern their season to search and their season to stop searching.

CROSS EXAMINATION – *Examined by the Cross*

1. *Have you ever had a season in which you believed God wanted you to search for someone or something?*
2. *Have you ever had a season in which you believed God wanted you to give up a search?*
3. *Natasha implies that God called Raymond to represent a client, but did not call Raymond to win. Do you agree with Natasha's logic? Why would God call a person to fight a losing battle?*
4. *Have you ever been called to fight a losing battle?*

Day 34

POSSIBLY GIFTED

"A time to keep and a time to throw away."
Ecclesiastes 3:6 NIV (in part)

"What is this?" Adalia questioned as she sorted through piles of paperwork in her husband's home office. Pablo's practice suffered greatly because of his lack of organization and the fact that his files had outgrown the small space in their home. This quarterly clean-up day helped the couple to maintain some control over the unmanageable files, while simultaneously helping them to keep their marriage peaceful and harmonious.

Staring at a crumpled pink sheet of paper, Pablo could only shake his head and laugh. The sheet was the carbon copy page of a document that he had kept for decades.

"When I was in ninth grade, one of my teachers, Mr. Lathrop, told me that I did not belong in his class. He read my writing assignment and told me that I should be in the gifted and talented classes. Mr. Lathrop even wrote a note for me to take to my parents," Pablo began.

Adalia patiently listened to her husband's prelude to an anecdote as she marked files for storage and files for shredding. Pablo narrated an account of the obstacles that school officials constructed to prevent him from entering the honor program.

Other parents simply submitted a form for entry into the gifted and talented courses; however, Chalisdale High School required Pablo to undertake two, three hour exams to prove he could handle the academic demands of the school honor program. He spent the morning taking a Comprehensive Language Arts/Social Studies Exam and the afternoon taking a Comprehensive Mathematics Exam.

"We were only two weeks into the school year, but the guidance counselors told my parents that I would be so far behind the 'truly gifted students' that it wasn't worth switching classes. They felt that I would only get bad grades and reduce my chances of going to a good college. Blah, blah, blah, just more reasons to discourage me from trying. So I took their exams and scored in the 99 percentile in each one. I scored higher than the honor kids throughout the country who took the exam," Pablo smirked as he reflected on the steps he had to take to become the first Latino in his high school honor program. The Guidance Counselor's Class Transfer sheet contained a note to Pablo's parents.

"Based on Pablo's test scores in the 99 percentile for the Comprehensive Mathematics and Language Arts/Social Studies Examinations, we have reason to believe that he *may possibly be gifted* and suited for the Chalisdale High School Honor's Program," Pablo quoted while reading the "may possibly be gifted" part with sarcastic emphasis. He referred to the sheet during tough times in college and law school. He even carried it in his pocket during the bar exam as a reminder that he could break through any barrier with God's help. Pablo Cabiya vowed to be defined by God instead of man.

"The note reminds me that even though people may try to place me in a particular class and limit me, God breaks all limits. If God gives me a gift then I'll always be gifted regardless of anyone's test or opinion," Pablo concluded.

"But do you still need that reminder, Honey? Is there anything left for you to prove?" Adalia asked while taking a subtle nod towards the recycling bin. Pablo had kept the pink sheet of paper for so long. His parents had the white cover sheet, but threw it away years ago while Pablo held onto the carbon copy believing the Guidance Counselor's mistake in sending him the copy to be a fortuitous error. The pink paper stood out and served as a great reminder and motivator.

The note inspired him when he needed it, but now it only served as a reminder of pain and obstruction. Pablo had enough souvenirs and awards of even greater accomplishments. The legal community knew that Pablo was definitely gifted, so there was no need to hold onto a note saying that he was "possibly gifted." The gifted attorney tossed the paper into the recycling bin. There was a time to keep it, but now it was time to throw it away.

CROSS EXAMINATION – *Examined by the Cross*

1. What souvenirs and memories are you holding onto?
2. Do they empower you or keep you in the past?
3. What should you keep? What should you throw away?
4. Should your decision be based on a season in your life or are there things that you should always hold onto regardless of your season?
5. Read the poem by Mother Teresa. Which stains are you required to erase in love? Which stains do you want erased?

"Love has a hem to her garment
That reaches the very dust.
It sweeps the stains
From the streets and lanes,
And because it can, it must."
Mother Teresa

Break-up and Make-up

"A time to tear and a time to mend."
Ecclesiastes 3:7 NIV (in part)

"Pooja, are you sure about this?" Anna asked for the third time. Anna remembered the lengthy conversation in which her client had ripped up the partnership agreement with Amit Patel three years ago. Pooja laughed gleefully on her mobile phone for the first time in months as she insisted that her attorney draft a new agreement with Mr. Patel. She admitted having been disappointed with Amit's spending, disorganization, and overall failure to make sound business decisions. Pooja acknowledged that she had made the right decision to tear up the partnership agreement to prevent any further loss; however, Pooja had always admired Amit's people skills and friendliness.

"Amit has a gift for marketing and developing business. I want to hire him to generate sales," Pooja stated while insisting that her attorney draft a marketing agreement.

"At least, hire him on a trial basis and pay him on commission. After all you've been through, he doesn't deserve a flat monthly fee," Anna advised.

"We've been through our season. I was right to fire him as a partner, because he was not a good partner. Now is the time for forgiveness and a new beginning. His failure as a partner was no less his fault than mine. He was not ready. He can be the right person when in the right position. He's brilliant at marketing," Pooja explained. Pooja, then, proceeded to discuss the importance of forgiveness and grace.

"Here comes the set-up," laughed Anna, "You never miss an opportunity to invite me to your church."

"Yet, you have never taken advantage of the opportunity. I'm sure lawyers spend a lot of time in fight mode and only see the other side as the adversary. I appreciate you for that, but Christ reminds us that our adversaries often know not what they do and sometimes we have to bridge people to ourselves," Pooja added.

"Don't put it all on me. You put me in fight mode. I remember your complaints. *Amit did this* and *Amit did that.* Ha! Ha! Ha! I'll go to your church. Just let me know when you have communion Sunday. I think I'll need a really big piece of bread for missed time," Anna laughed.

"So funny. . . you're crazy. . . one little piece will do. His body was broken, but now the body of Christ must be unified. This is the season for mending," Pooja declared.

<u>CROSS EXAMINATION</u> - *Examined by the Cross*

1. *What is something that should be torn out of your life? Do you need help from God or from others to tear that thing or person out of your life?*
2. *What is something that should be mended in your life? Do you need help from God or from others to mend that thing or relationship in your life?*
3. *Have you experienced the two kinds of blessings that are addressed in the quote below?*

"Some people bless you when they come into your life;
some people bless you when they exit your life."
Jentezen Franklin

Day 36

You have Nothing to add

"A time to be silent and a time to speak."
Ecclesiastes 3:7 NIV (in part)

"You have nothing to add," advised Warner Stanton. Warner had a great reputation as a criminal defense attorney, and deserved to be trusted by his client; however, Erica wanted to tell her side of the story. She loved her daughter too much to ever try to hurt her, yet her attorney advised her not to testify.

"But, I didn't do anything. I'm innocent," Erica pleaded in resentment of the appearance of hiding behind her attorney. According to Erica's ex-husband, Calvin, their daughter, Stacy, complained of foot pains during his weekend visitation. Calvin took Stacy to a hospital which identified several hairline fractures within the nine year olds' feet and hands. The doctors made no claim of abuse; however, Calvin alleged that Erica either abused or neglected their daughter. He believed that she either caused the injuries or should have discovered them and sought medical attention for their daughter.

"The State has no evidence against you other than the fact that your daughter had fractures. There were no bruises and no testimony from your daughter that you ever beat her. There was no testimony to prove that you ever neglected her. You don't have to explain how the fractures occurred. They have to prove that you abused your child either intentionally or by neglect. Anything you say would only present the appearance of a cover up or ignorance," Warner advised.

Erica never wanted to be like the politicians who hid behind their attorneys in the midst of a scandal. She believed that her daughter probably suffers from the same bone disease that affected her Aunt Pamela. Erica had no proof of the bone disease and because of the temporary protective order, she had not been able to take her daughter to a specialist. Her attorney reminded her that she was emotional and had grabbed his arm during their discussion. Erica's testimony could cause the judge to see her as being violent and untruthful. Despite her frustration, she accepted the advice of counsel and did not testify.

"We have nothing to add, your Honor," Warner informed the court. The judge quickly denied the request for a protective order after finding no evidence of abuse.

Many believe that Christians should speak the truth at all times; in fact, some assert that silence shows cowardice. If Christians have power and authority from God, then they should speak up and glorify Him at all times, right?

Wisdom is best revealed through those who know the proper season to speak and not to speak. In seasons where discernment is needed, Christians should definitely refer to Jesus as their example. Jesus remained silent before Herod[9], yet answered Pilate[10]. He did not speak in vain. Every word spoken glorified the Father. Jesus remained silent before Herod to fulfill the scripture that he was led like a sheep to the slaughter.[11] He did not ramble before Herod or try to talk His way out of the crucifixion. Whereas to the contrary, Jesus spoke to Pilate to inform the governor that man had no power to resist the Father's will.

In this era of social media, people feel compelled to express their opinions on every news event or celebrity scandal. Christians waste their credibility whenever they speak in vain. In the church, pastors often ruin great sermons by inserting political views as opposed to being spirit led.

---

[9] **Luke 23:7-10**

[10] **Luke 23:1-5**

[11] **Isaiah 53:7**

Solomon, in his wisdom, advises the body of Christ that there is a time to speak and a time to be silent. Christians should remain silent whenever they have nothing to add.

CROSS EXAMINATION – *Examined by the Cross*

1. *Have you ever heard a great sermon ruined because a pastor injected a political view or personal opinion that had nothing to do with the gospel?*
2. *Have you ever changed your view of someone who posted an opinion or inappropriate joke on social media?*
3. *Have you ever thought about how others perceive you when you make statements outside of the word of God?*
4. *Would you have been able to trust your attorney and remain silent if you were accused of child abuse? Isn't there something wrong with being silent when we have the truth within us?*

"All our words will be useless unless they come from within. Words that do not give the light of Christ increase the darkness."

Mother Teresa

Day 37

SOMETIMES IT'S OKAY TO BE A HATER

"A time to love and a time to hate."
Ecclesiastes 3:8 NIV (in part)

"They're just haters, Karen! I'm going to wear what I wanna wear," griped Tabitha as she stretched her legs across the family room couch. Tabitha had been so enthralled in her conversation that she did not notice that her father's car pulled into the driveway.

At 4:43 pm, Joel McCabe entered his home and directed a slightly annoyed frown to Tabitha to take her feet off the couch. Joel usually came home after seven o'clock on weekdays; however, he stood in front of her while the evening sun shone through the family room window. This would be the first time in years that he arrived home before his wife.

"Oh, it's just my father walking in. Anyways, I'm just saying, everybody expresses themselves differently. If you don't have the body, then don't hate. If you have the body, then you wear what you want to wear. Women don't need to hide it or hate it," Tabitha reasoned.

Joel looked at his fifteen year old daughter in total disbelief and disgust. *"Was this the outfit that she wore to school?"* he wondered. He pondered why the teachers allowed her to stay in school the entire day without calling him. She wore a midriff top with a tight short skirt that revealed too much of the contours of her young body. Joel could not believe that Tabitha owned theses clothes, or even worse, wore these rags without him or Becky noticing.

"Tabitha, why are you naked?" Joel asked as he dropped his trial bag.

"Karen, I'm going to have to go. My dad just added himself to the hater list," Tabitha fired. The adolescent knew that she had been caught by her father in an inappropriate outfit, but she also felt that her clothes were part of her identity and expression. Tabitha normally changed before her parents got home, but her father had gotten home early today.

"Ok, then I'm a hater. I hate that outfit. You can't dress like that. You have to respect yourself. You have to command respect from others. . . ," Joel began his opening argument.

"How hypocritical! You aren't supposed to hate anything. You're a Christian. God is love. You're so busted, Dad!" Tabitha argued.

"That's partially true. . . God *loves*. God *loves* purity. God *loves* holiness. There are also things that God *hates*. In the Bible, God says 'Jacob I love, Esau I *hated*'. Jude wrote 'save others by snatching them from the fire; to others show mercy, mixed with fear--*hating* even the clothing stained by corrupted flesh'. We are to love one another, but there are things that we should *hate*," Joel finished.

He explained that he *hated* the fact that girls who dressed a certain way garnered more attention. He *hated* the fact that so many teen celebrities wore so little clothing. He *loved* this time in his daughter's life in which her innocence remained uncorrupted. He *loved* the fact that his daughter saw herself as a princess and desired a prince more than a lover; however, he wanted the boys to see a princess not a prostitute.

Joel concluded, "Someday you will be a parent. To be a good parent, you will *love* a lot of things, but there are some things you will have to *hate*. You cannot truly love anyone without hating anything that comes against that love."

"You win. I *hate* lectures, but *love* peace," joked Tabitha as she tossed a throw pillow at her father. She darted up the stairs and closed the door to her room. Joel laughed and thanked God that he still had his little girl even though she was tempted to dress like someone else and something else.

CROSS Examination – *Examined by the Cross*

1. Do you agree or disagree with Joel's view that you cannot love without hating things that come against that love?
2. Is it possible to hate something without sinning?
3. Aren't we supposed to love everyone and perhaps hate their actions instead of the person?
4. Have you experienced seasons of love and hate?
5. What is the context in which God says that "He hated Esau"? Is this hate or hyperbole? Was this merely a figure of speech or an exaggeration?
6. See Deuteronomy 12:31, 16:21, Psalm 11:5, Proverbs 6:16, and Malachi 2:16. In these scriptures, what is the context in which the writer says that God hates? Is this hate or hyperbole?

Day 38

The Enemy Advances While You Stand Still

"A time for war and a time for peace."
Ecclesiastes 3:8 NIV (in part)

"You just don't get it. There's a war going on whether you choose to fight or not," Tiffany shrieked. Tiffany made so many efforts to avoid sounding like an attorney who was bloodthirsty for litigation. Tiffany could take no more of Mr. Bempong's incessant excuses for his partner, Wendell Cooke's, lack of ethics.

Darren Bempong owned a fitness club franchise with Wendell Cooke. Darren initially became concerned when Wendell started disappearing for hours at a time. Instead of working at the main location as agreed, Wendell would be inaccessible most work days. He often claimed to be working at other sites, but no one could confirm his claims.

For months, Darren ignored complaints from employees who repeatedly informed him of Wendell's backbiting and intent to start another company. Wendell frequently said horrible things about Darren to foster distrust and to get key staff to question his competency. Darren recently discovered substantial amounts of inventory and funds missing from several locations.

"You're like a wife who thinks she'll ruin the marriage if she calls out her husband's infidelity. Do you need any more evidence to know he's unfaithful? He's stealing from you and starting another company. If you want to bury your head in the sand like an ostrich, then you'll prove his point that you're too incompetent to run a business," Tiffany warned. The attorney collected billable hours regardless of whether clients took her advice; in fact, she made more money off of the ones who failed to heed her warnings. However, she hated to see clients suffer needlessly.

"I tried talking to him so many times. He denies starting a business. I didn't want to start a fight. We grew up together. Christians should not be fighting. I can't believe he's doing this to me," Mr. Bempong sulked.

"There are wars throughout the Bible. God not only called His children to fight, but there were times when He commanded His people to wipe everyone out and to destroy everything. You need to file an injunction to stop him from liquidating your company. You should also consider filing criminal charges," advised Tiffany.

Tiffany reminded Mr. Bempong that great heroes of the faith such as Moses, Deborah, Joshua, and David were warriors and that sometimes peace comes by no other way than war. The attorney could not understand why he stood still as the enemy advanced. "Refusing to fight doesn't necessary take you out of one, it just means you're taking hits," Tiffany argued.

After the meeting, Tiffany accompanied Mr. Bempong to the nearest police station to report the theft of equipment that had been transported to Wendell Cooke's new gym. The partnership agreement specifically precluded any seizure of property, thus giving the officers grounds to make the arrest.

What should Christians do when the peaceful option has failed? Children of God must seek the Lord for discernment of when to turn the other cheek and when to go to battle. God told Joshua multiple times to be strong and courageous.[12] One cannot hold an absolute position as a hawk or a dove when dealing with the enemy; moreover, every Christian must respond in due season to the Lord's call to pursue peace or to fight a war.

CROSS EXAMINATION – *Examined by the Cross*

1. *There are some people who avoid conflict as much as possible and then there are some who readily engage. Do you fall to either extreme?*
2. *Have you had seasons of war in your life? What happened?*
3. *Have you had seasons of peace in your life? How was it established? How long did it last?*
4. *Did you see God in your seasons of war?*
5. *Did you see God in your seasons of peace?*

---

[12] **Joshua Chapter 1**

CHAPTER 4

TRIALS OF THE PRAISE

"I will praise the LORD, who counsels me;
even at night my heart instructs me.
I have set the LORD always before me.
Because he is at my right hand,
I will not be shaken."
Psalm 16:7-8 NIV

Day 39

MATERIAL WITNESS

"He put a new song in my mouth,
a hymn of praise to our God.
Many will see and fear and
put their trust in the LORD."
Psalm 40:3 - NIV

K adienne Bosino created one big loose end for Vadim Alkaev. One Sunday afternoon, Kadienne entered the office to finish work that should have been completed on Friday. Instead of finding a quiet empty office, Mr. Alkaev's trustworthy secretary observed her boss standing over a dead body and yelling at strange looking men to clean up the mess.

Fortunately for her, no one noticed her exit. Unfortunately for her, life would never be the same. Kadienne immediately contacted the police and Vadim was arrested within minutes. The State intended to present Kadienne as a material witness. A "material witness" is someone capable of determining the outcome of a trial.

Within days, Kadienne received an unusual phone call from her best friend, Edna, requesting to meet for lunch. Edna had never invited Kadienne to lunch before and refused to explain her urgency.

A waitress led Kadienne to a booth in the rear of the restaurant occupied by Edna and a well-dressed older man. The well-dressed man introduced himself to Kadienne as Alfred Lagunov, Vadim Alkaev's criminal defense attorney. Mr. Lagunov offered Kadienne one million dollars to settle her civil lawsuit for emotional distress against Mr. Alkaev.

"It must have been traumatic to go to your workplace and see the things that you saw. The check should cover your damages," Alfred sympathized.

"I didn't file a lawsuit against Mr. Alkaev. There must be some mistake," Kadienne said as she backed away from the booth. She was shocked that her best friend put her in contact with anyone who knew Mr. Alkaev. Then, Kadienne realized that they either threatened Edna or bribed her. Alkaev's check was a veiled bribe for her to leave the country and to forget about testifying at the murder trial.

"Life is short. You should enjoy yours. I understand that you're Dominican. You should go back to your home country. Why live here in fear of deportation? Why live in fear of other things that could happen if you stay?" the attorney hinted. Kadienne froze. First, he threatened to have her deported from the country and then he gave a less subtle threat to her life if she testified.

Kadienne took Mr. Lagunov's card and pretended to consider the offer. She quickly gathered her purse and mobile phone as she left the restaurant. Too frightened to return to her apartment, Kadienne entered witness protection and spent the next seven months in a safe house in Oxford, Nebraska. The secretary informant occasionally regretted her decision to testify during the twenty-two hour drive from her Manhattan apartment to Oxford with federal officers; however, her faith in God brought blessed assurance.

Mr. Lagunov aggressively cross-examined her at trial. He tried to intimidate her about her immigration status, but her work visa could be extended. He lied about the meeting at the restaurant and suggested that Kadienne demanded a one million dollar payoff to extort Vadim Alkaev. He even attempted to undermine her credibility with testimony from a scared Edna Branch.

Despite all of the theatrics and attacks, Kadienne felt at peace. The power of God's Holy Spirit filled her body the moment she raised her hand and made an oath to tell the truth, the whole truth, and nothing but the truth. The jury convicted Vadim Alkaev of first degree murder. As the media covered the story, the Major Crimes Unit of the New York Police Department received a boost of support from other witnesses who were inspired by Kadienne to come forward.

"I had to tell the police about the rape in my complex, because of Kadienne. It's like she messed up my conscience when she came forward. I'm like more afraid of God than anyone who wants to kill me for snitchin," said Carmelo Welkins, a witness for the prosecution who caught the Kadienne wave in Manhattan.

Kadienne even changed Alfred Lagunov's life. Her testimony set his conscience ablaze. He realized that he had sunk very low to intimidate a murder witness. After the Alkaev case, Lagunov started teaching paralegal courses at a community college and occasionally volunteered for the Innocence Project to make amends for his disreputable practice.

Kadienne made a tremendous sacrifice to present her testimony. She overcame fear and anxiety because she knew the importance of her words. Christians have a testimony of even greater significance. The people of God know of the life, death, and resurrection of Jesus Christ. Christians own a testimony that will set captives free and which will glorify our Heavenly Father. We are *material witnesses* capable of determining the eternal outcome for countless generations of people.

CROSS EXAMINATION - *Examined by the Cross*

1. Did you know that you are a material witness capable of determining a person's eternal outcome?
2. Read Psalm 40:3 - What testimony, song, or praise will you offer so that many will see Him, fear Him, and put their trust in Him?
3. Have you ever testified in the face of opposition and threat like Kadienne? Has it changed your life as it changed Kadienne? Did it change others?
4. Why does Revelation 12:11 say that they overcame the devil by the blood of the Lamb and by the word of their testimony? How do we overcome by our testimony? How is our testimony a threat to Satan and demonic forces?

"I'm against sin. I'll kick it as long as I have a foot. I'll fight it as long as I have a fist. I'll butt it as long as I have a head.
I'll bite it as long as I've got a tooth.
And when I'm old and fistless and footless and toothless,
I'll gum it till I go home to Glory and it goes home to perdition."
Billy Sunday

Day 40

MAGNIFY THE LORD!

**"O magnify the LORD with me,
and let us exalt his name together."
Psalm 34:3 KJV**

Greg Patterson could not believe his eyes as he walked with his client to Union Station. The attorney became captivated by a homeless man in a long white sheet singing hymns at the top of his voice in front of the Washington, DC metro station. The man had the worst voice that he had ever heard, yet praised God with all of His might. Some people laughed at the Psalmist while others simply ignored him. Greg thought about ignoring the seemingly half-crazed man as well.

Greg suddenly felt God tugging on his heart. He remembered Jesus' admonishment in Matthew 10:32, "Whoever acknowledges me before others, I will also acknowledge before my Father in heaven." The experienced attorney smiled at his client and said, "He's alright! I respect his conviction and heart." Greg immediately dropped a few dollars into the cardboard box labeled "offering" and advised the man to continue giving God the glory.

As the vagrant thanked Greg, a whiff of the man's foul odor also greeted the attorney. The Psalmist introduced himself and opened his hymnal to "What a Mighty God We Serve" and asked Greg and his client to join him in worshipping the Lord.

Greg thought he had been courageous in stepping out to publicly acknowledge himself as a Christian. The attorney had never sang hymns outside of church. He had a client with him and did not want to make his client feel uncomfortable.

"O magnify the Lord with me, and let us exalt his name together," the vagrant invited.

"I'm sorry, brother. I'm on the run, but keep lifting Him up," advised Greg as he politely retreated away from the extended hymnal that the vagrant attempted to share.

"Okay, I'll ask him, Lord. Hmmm, what's your name, my friend?" asked the homeless man as he tried to keep his sheet from blowing away. The vagrant appeared to be listening to a voice before asking his question.

"Greg. . . like Gregory," stated the attorney becoming more confident in front of his client now that singing was no longer at issue.

"That's interesting. 'Greg' means watchman. Stay on the watch! You are a watchman for God!" declared the Psalmist.

Greg thought he had stepped forward for Christ by encouraging the brother and giving him money. Greg felt that his bad voice would have misrepresented God and even turned people away. He further rationalized that he had a client and work to do. Yet, none of these excuses absolved Greg of his deep guilt and shame. *Greg was the vagrant.* Even though Greg had a nice residence in the suburbs, he felt homeless and lost after denying God.

As he rode the metro home that night, Greg thought about his encounter with the homeless man and how awesome it would have been to join his brother in song at Union Station during the busiest time of the day to magnify God. God is infinite and incapable of being magnified, but he could have magnified the Lord in the eyes of the people. He could have legitimized his brother's praise and joy. The homeless man wasn't crazy. He boldly ministered to thousands that day. Greg replayed the day over and over in his mind with a better ending in which he had been fearless.

If he had magnified the Lord with the man perhaps someone else may have joined in or even been saved. Greg thought about these things and vowed to accept more invitations to praise the Lord and to be a person who invited others too.

Greg's most important job is to serve God instead of his client or even his reputation. At home, he opened the Bible unintentionally to Ezekiel 33 and read his charge to be a watchman for the people of God. The Lord promises a punishment for the watchman who fails to sound the alarm for the people. Greg vowed to be prepared to magnify the Lord in the eyes of men and women regardless of convenience or critique.

CROSS EXAMINATION – *Examined by the Cross*

1. *What does it mean to you when people talk about magnifying the Lord? Are you actually making Him bigger or just making Him bigger in the eyes of others?*
2. *Where do you draw the line between <u>showing your faith</u> and just <u>making your faith a show</u>?*
3. *Have you ever been in a position to show your faith in public?*
4. *Have you ever felt Greg's shame in cowering from the faith? Have you ever denied Christ as Peter had done in Matthew 26:69-75? Did you ever feel restored like Peter?*

Day 41

Bad Counsel

**"Blessed is the man who does not walk in the counsel
of the wicked or stand in the way of sinners
or sit in the seat of mockers.
But his delight is in the law of the LORD
and on his law he meditates day and night."
Psalm 1:1-2 - NIV**

Victoria Ogletree grew tired of waiting for Judge Ohlman to make his way through the juvenile court docket. There were times that the learned Judge seemed to be highly efficient while other times the judge spent excessive energy yelling at the youth and even the parents. Some of the youth faced juvenile detention for violating probation.

Victoria paid special attention to Judge Ohlman's unbridled fury against Tommy Ellis and Tommy's mother. Tommy could have avoided twelve months in juvenile detention if he simply completed fifty hours of community service between May and July.

"Mrs. Ellis, I still don't understand why your son could not complete my community service request?" inquired Judge Ohlman.

"Judge, he wanted to do it, but I can't drive him to community service all the time. . . I have to work too," said Lula Ellis.

"You have a church within walking distance to your home. We have organizations that will pick up young healthy men who are willing to help. Yet, you did nothing to keep your son out of juvi!" Judge Ohlman erupted on the parent prior to turning to Tommy.

"I tried telling her that I had to do community service, but she was like. . .you don't have to worry about it cuz I can't take you," added Tommy.

"Well, I'm sorry young man. You had some bad counsel. I have a feeling that you had a lot of bad advice growing up. I have a feeling that you are at a disadvantage due to a lack of parenting. However, you know how to read, write, and understand the English language. You were here when I told you what to do, so now you have twelve months in juvenile detention to think about the importance of following the law instead of what other people, even a parent, tell you to do!" snapped Judge Ohlman.

Even though, Victoria agreed with the message that Ohlman sent Tommy and to everyone in the court room, her heart went out to the young man. Victoria called Brennan Qatora, a colleague from her firm, to reach out to Tommy and to visit him. Brennan mentored Tommy and gave him good counsel about personal responsibility, dealing with life's disappointments, and knowing and trusting God's plan.

Sin came into this world because of bad counsel. The serpent advised Eve to eat forbidden fruit and Eve advised Adam to do likewise. God is the ultimate judge and has given all of humanity a probationary period to avoid the ultimate sentence of eternal damnation. By accepting Jesus Christ as Lord and Savior, his children can obtain mercy.

Many people had the good fortune of being born and raised in the church; however, the numbers are increasing in each following generation of those who have no background in the church. Parents are increasingly raising children to be more secular in a secular world. Despite this fact, God will hold every individual accountable who fails to accept His grace. Everyone must study the word and have a personal relationship with Jesus Christ or take a risk of relying on bad counsel. God will hold us accountable if we fail to listen to Him.

CROSS EXAMINATION - *Examined by the Cross*

1. *Do you have good counsel in your life?*
2. *Do you understand that God will hold you accountable for your decisions regardless of what others may have advised you?*
3. *Do you realize that He will hold you accountable regardless of your background or experiences?*

Day 42

IN The MORNING

"For his anger endureth but a moment;
in his favour is life;
weeping may endure for a night,
but joy cometh in the morning."
Psalm 30:5 - KJV[13]

Brennan enjoyed his meetings with Tommy in juvenile detention. After two months had passed, Brennan decided to file a motion to the court to ask Judge Ohlman to reconsider the twelve month sentence. There was no question that Tommy defied the order. There was no question that he was wrong to listen to his mother instead of completing community service on time. There was no question that Tommy was not worthy of the grace that Judge Ohlman gave him the first time and he was even less worthy of another chance. Yet, Brennan wanted to demonstrate Tommy's remorse and transformation to the court. Brennan challenged Tommy to be of good cheer and to trust that God's favor and forgiveness extends beyond his sins.

---

[13] "Favor" is spelled with a "u" in the King James Version of the Bible.

Tommy struggled to see beyond his shame and remained blinded by his guilt. He whipped himself mentally for being foolish enough to get into a fight with a classmate over something as trivial as a football game. In a moment of anger, he assaulted a boy for teasing him after his team lost. Tommy sat in disbelief in juvenile detention that he could be an even bigger imbecile for not doing community service. He had to agree with Judge Ohlman's reprimand since there were numerous community service opportunities available which did not require a car; in fact, he watched friends complete their obligations after school and could have joined them at any time.

Brennan's interest in Tommy and willingness to make several visits to juvenile detention helped to erase some of the shame. Each visit from Brennan provided proof to Tommy that the teenager had value. Brennan shared the gospel with his mentee with specific emphasis on the fact that God values Tommy and has a future for him.

In the hearing, Brennan challenged Judge Ohlman to allow anger to give way to mercy that grace may abide. Judge Ohlman appreciated Brennan's petition in the midst of his fading anger. Brennan showed the court that Tommy would be under the care of new counsel: counsel that would help the youth make better decisions. Tommy now had legal counsel and most importantly the Wonderful Counselor in Jesus Christ.

Judge Ohlman ordered Tommy's release and reinstated the terms of probation with the previous community service requirements. Instead of following the new order, Tommy completed twice the requested hours.

The Almighty God sits in heaven ready, willing, and able to pronounce judgment in response to any action and inaction, deed and misdeed, and misfeasance and malfeasance. Jesus Christ is a counselor who reminds the people of God of their true value even when they are in sin. The Savior reminds everyone daily, through His word and through the Spirit, that the Father is just, merciful, and forgiving. Praise the Lord for Brennan's willingness to share this message to Tommy! Praise the Lord for Tommy's willingness to receive it!

Always be willing to acknowledge your sins and shortcomings. Always be willing to petition Him with pleas for mercy and forgiveness. His anger is momentary, His favor is eternal, and His love endures forever!

In the morning – there is forgiveness!
In the morning – there is restoration!
In the morning – there is joy!
In the morning – there is praise!

CROSS EXAMINATION – *Examined by the Cross*

1. *Identify one error in your life in which you have yet to forgive yourself. Why are you still bothered by that mistake?*
2. *Identify one sin that someone has committed against you. Why are you still bothered by that sin?*
3. *Does your sin prevent you from being productive?*
4. *Do you feel any urgency to accept grace or to tell others about His grace?*

"I preached. . .as a dying man to dying men."
Richard Baxter

Day 43

ENVY NOT THE WICKED

**"But as for me, my feet had almost slipped;
I had nearly lost my foothold.
For I envied the arrogant
when I saw the prosperity of the wicked."
Psalm 73:2-3 - NIV**

Judge Mei Zhen Wang looked at the stacks of files on her desk. Even though she had started at 6:00 am, there was no way for her to become 100% familiarized with the morning docket by 9:00 am. Judge Wang often hated the fact that she had such a conscience and worked harder than the other judges. Judge Crachett in Courtroom 1 often laughed that he did not bother to review files before a hearing and makes decisions based only on what is presented at trial. Judge Hofstrom's clerks indicated that she often flips a coin underneath the bench to decide case outcomes. According to one bailiff, Judge Raspberry gets kickbacks from the larger law firms. There were three firms that he would never rule against.

"Life would be so much easier sometimes if I weren't a Christian. Why do I have to have a conscience?" Judge Wang thought while feeling sorry for herself. She worked twice the hours as the other judges while having less to show for it.

Judge Wang and Judge Raspberry were up for election this year and Wang lacked the finances and the team to campaign. Governor Palmer appointed her to the position a few years ago after the death of Judge Haskins, but she knew nothing about campaigning. The other judges practically campaigned from the bench and made decisions that helped their constituents.

Now, it appeared that she would probably lose her seat on the bench. Wang felt terribly and repented for envying the wicked and the corrupted. To change the atmosphere of depression and covetousness in the office, she pulled up a website of a Christian radio station that played commercial free music. Her joy increased with each song as the Holy Spirit renewed her mind, restored her faith, and rejuvenated her strength.

In the midst of her worship, a news clip ran across the bottom of the screen indicating that Detective Dudley Maddox had been arrested for robbing and assaulting drug dealers who competed with his trafficking. Every closed case involving Detective Maddox would now be reviewed closely. Wang remembered that Judge Raspberry had dismissed all evidence against Maddox in a brutality case. That case would definitely come under severe scrutiny and rule out an election campaign.

Wang apologized to God again, "Even if they don't get justice down here, I know you will bring everyone to justice. I have no right worrying about how you do your job."

Whenever evil succeeds, good men and women may question God. They may question God's existence, God's concern for justice, and even God's love for His children. Scripture warns the people of God against envying the wicked. Temporary circumstances should never shake the foundation of faith. Our Father promises reward for the righteous and punishment for the wicked.

Just like the Psalmist, Judge Wang's understanding did not come from an intellectual breakthrough or a theological epiphany, but an encounter with the spirit.

Psalm 73:16-17 records the encounter:

> "When I tried to understand all this [intern],
> it was oppressive to me
> *till I entered the sanctuary of God;*
> then I understood their final destiny."
> **Psalm 73:16-17 – NIV emphasis added**

God made mankind in His image so Christians naturally grieve injustice. Every Christian should seek God with their whole heart in times of discouragement. The sanctuary may be a church building, but it can also be any place where you enter His presence. Judge Wang found a sanctuary in Christian music during her time of distress.

CROSS EXAMINATION – *Examined by the Cross*

1. Is there a particular injustice that you are aware of that affects your belief in God?
2. Does injustice make you doubt God's power or distrust His goodness for allowing it to occur?
3. What does the Psalmist mean in Psalm 73 by saying that he had almost slipped? Do you believe that Judge Wang almost slipped from envying the wicked? How have you almost slipped or actually slipped while envying the wicked?
4. Read the quote below. Meditate on the fact that if we keep our minds on God, then we keep our minds in heaven. If we are in heaven, then we have nothing to envy. If we have God, then we have no one to envy.

"Wherever God is, there is Heaven."
St. Teresa of Avila

By Gregory D. Yancey, Esq.

Day 44

A Steadfast Spirit

"Create in me a pure heart, O God, and
renew a steadfast spirit within me.
Do not cast me from your presence or
take your Holy Spirit from me."
Psalm 51:10-11 - NIV

Amira Bachman never could catch her anonymous benefactor. Every December, she received a special gift. Some years she would find clothes and toys on the porch for the children and for herself. Then, there was the time that envelopes filled with cash awaited her in the mailbox. This year topped all previous years. The dealership sent her a letter stating that her car note had been paid in full.

The gifts started coming the year after her husband, Caedmon, had been killed by Jibril Bennett, a drunk driver. Amira always wondered if the gifts came from the driver, from Caedmon's ghost, from a guardian angel, or from Jesus. She never suspected that the gifts came from Jibril Bennett's attorney, Byron Calliste.

Byron represented Jibril in a Driving While Intoxicated Case (DWI) case years before the accident that killed Caedmon. Byron lied to the judge by stating that Jibril had never had a DWI. Byron knew that Jibril had a DWI in another state but did not disclose it to the court. If Byron had disclosed the prior DWI: Jibril would have lost his license and served jail time, Caedmon Bachman would be alive, and Amira would not be a widow.

Byron does not send ongoing gifts to the Bachmans solely out of guilt. The gifts remind Byron of the importance of having a steadfast spirit and always being right with God. As David indicates throughout Psalm 51, there are severe consequences for even momentary broken fellowship with God.

David, a man after God's own heart, broke a series of commandments in his pursuit of Bathsheba. In lusting for a married woman and killing her husband, he committed idolatry (First and Second Commandment), dishonored his parents and the family name (Fifth Commandment), murdered (Sixth Commandment), committed adultery (Seventh Commandment), stole (Eighth Commandment), bore false witness (Ninth Commandment), and coveted (Tenth Commandment). If any of these actions happened on the Sabbath, then he violated the Fourth Commandment as well.

David remained on the throne because of his confession of sin and desire to maintain a pure heart and steadfast spirit, but there were severe consequences of his sins: Uriah's death, the death of David's child, and David's kingdom began to hemorrhage.

Byron knew his sins were forgiven, yet he still sought to provide for a widow and her family to keep his heart pure. Of course it is far better to avoid the pitfalls of sin, but whenever a Christian falls he or she should climb up and climb out immediately for restored fellowship with the Lord. Without this fellowship and a steadfast spirit within, there is no life.

CROSS EXAMINATION - *Examined by the Cross*

1. *What are the possible consequences in your life, if you do not have a pure heart?*
2. *What are the possible consequences in your life, if you do not have a steadfast spirit or a Holy Spirit filled life?*
3. *When you do something wrong, what do you do to feel right with God?*
4. *Are you a person with a heavy conscience or a light conscience?*

Day 45

A Multi-Cultural God

"The heavens declare the glory of God;
the skies proclaim the work of his hands.
Day after day they pour forth speech;
night after night they display knowledge.
There is no speech or language where
their voice is not heard."
Psalm 19:1-3 NIV

Augustine stood prepared to "miss out on a good time", yet he had no regrets at the annual conference. While all of his colleagues from the Entertainment Law Bar Association basked in the Hawaiian nightlife after the final workshop session, he could not help but to be intrigued by a flier for a prayer service within miles of the hotel. He could not pass up the opportunity to fellowship with godly people on his first and only trip to a Hawaiian island. In fact, he felt compelled to invite some of his colleagues to consider the Hawaiian church over Hawaiian clubs on their last night in paradise.

"No thanks, I'm not into organized religion. I can't see God throwing people into hell who do not know Jesus. The concept of Jesus does not fit into everyone's culture," said Horace, a sports agent, as he declined Augustine's invitation to the prayer service.

After a short cab ride, Augustine entered a small church to hear beautiful tribal music. He received warm nods from the hosts and the congregants as they went in and out of a number of prayers. Even though he entered alone, he did not feel alone.

Occasionally the hosts would say the name, "Jesus" in English; however, the church leaders often spoke in their native dialect. Augustine recognized the melody to hymns such as "Amazing Grace" and "Precious Lord" while his ears enjoyed singing in a different language. Augustine welcomed the familiar presence of God in the midst of an unfamiliar setting.

God is creator of the universe, thus universal. He understands cultural differences more than anyone. The heavens declare His glory and He constantly speaks to everyone under the same sky. Psalm 19:1-4 declares that creation evidences God's work, God's speech, and God's knowledge. Humanity only needs to listen.

The evidence of His existence and sovereignty had been encoded within mankind's physical and spiritual DNA as well. The origin of Christianity, as chronicled from Genesis through Revelation, spans multiple continents with people from every tongue, tribe, and nation. Make no mistake, "there is no speech or language" where the knowledge and understanding of the Lord remains unheard. God and godly people can be found throughout the world. Horace was wrong. People throughout the world know, understand, and accept Jesus as their Lord and Savior. All Christians belong to a multi-cultural God and represent the kingdom culture.

CROSS EXAMINATION – *Examined by the Cross*

1. *How do you respond to the argument that Jesus cannot be the only way, because some people do not know about Him?*
2. *How can God be multi-cultural? How does Christianity transcend cultural boundaries?*
3. *What does Psalm 19:3 mean by "[t]here is no speech or language where their voice is not heard?"*

"We can hear children singing:
In Christ there is no East or West.
In Him no North or South,
But one great Fellowship of Love
Throughout the whole wide world.
This is the only way."
Rev. Dr. Martin Luther King, Jr.

By Gregory D. Yancey, Esq.

Day 46

STATUTORY GUARDRAILS

The *law* of the LORD is perfect, reviving the soul.
The *statutes* of the LORD are trustworthy,
making wise the simple.
The *precepts* of the LORD are right, giving joy to the heart.
The *commands* of the LORD are radiant, giving light to the eyes.
The *fear* of the LORD is pure, enduring forever.
The *ordinances* of the LORD are sure and altogether righteous.
They are more precious than gold, than much pure gold;
they are sweeter than honey from the comb.
By them is your servant warned;
in keeping them there is great reward.
Psalm 19:7-11 (emphasis added) - NIV

"Law school would only take one year if we didn't have so many dumb laws, but then again what would the lawyers do?" joked Senator Dacek. Deanna Brondello, Dacek's attorney, cringed every time her boss made fun of the legal profession. The two matriculated through law school together and fully knew the virtues of the law and the rationale behind the complexities of the legal system, yet Dacek ran a campaign designed to ignite his constituency. The senator enjoyed telling lawyer jokes and bashing bureaucrats for making Big Government even bigger. After one campaign event, Deanna warned her boss as his attorney and good friend against denouncing authority. She feared that his rhetoric invited bitterness, lawlessness, and disrespect for all authority.

There may be legitimate reasons to want smaller government and fewer laws. Laws often stifle people. Laws can cause gridlock. The tax codes can be complicated. The regulations for registering and operating a business may even scare people from entrepreneurship. There are laws that many hate and that people hate to follow; however, laws also offer protection, wisdom, and morality.

God provides *laws, statutes, precepts, commands, ordinances* which are invaluable guardrails that protect lives and provide tremendous rewards. Even the most careful driver benefits from guardrails. Christians do not always see the big pictured purpose of rules and regulation; however, they must trust God's wisdom and love for his children. King David rejoiced in the warnings and the rewards that can be harvested from God's law. Christians should do likewise.

CROSS EXAMINATION - *Examined by the Cross*

1. *Identify a warning and a reward that you received from scripture?*
2. *Identify a warning and a reward that someone else received from scripture?*

Day 47

STOP LYING!

**"The LORD is my shepherd I shall not be in want. . .
You prepare a table before me in the presence of my enemies.
You anoint my head with oil; my cup overflows."
Psalm 23:1-5 in part - NIV**

"C'mon, Jamal. . . if you won the lottery, what would you buy?" asked Marsada while savoring the artichoke crab flatbread. The associates ate like kings and queens during the quarterly law firm happy hours; this one would be no different.

"Nothing, I'm okay with the house and the car that God has blessed me with," responded Jamal.

"Stop lying!" screamed Marsada and Daphne not realizing that their voices carried.

Jamal explained that his car had always been reliable and that he genuinely liked his neighborhood. He admitted that he might travel more, but for the most part he loved his life. He enjoyed practicing law at the firm.

"I have a good reputation in this area as an immigration attorney and I believe I am making a difference. I would continue practicing at least for another five years even if I won the lottery," concluded Jamal.

"Stop lying!" jumped in Mitch and Roger as they made their way to the crab balls and shrimp hors d'oeuvres. Mitch called Jamal out for being a kiss up. Roger admitted that he would resign the day they took his photo in front of the big check.

"Why is it so hard to believe that I'm satisfied with my life? I'd donate more money to the poor. I'd help people in need, but I don't see much that I would change. My cup runneth over," Jamal continued to litigate his point as more co-workers joined their discussion. People drank and ate freely from the buffet lines as the caterers continued to bring out more food.

"You need to stop lying!" snarled Marsada. I hear the holier than thou, pious Christian rhetoric, but let's be real – you'd be a baller: new car, new house, new everything!"

"It's not a holier than thou thing, I'm just happy. God has blessed me. I have already won the lottery. I shall not want," Jamal said. Jamal whispered to one caterer to keep bringing crab balls to the table for Mitch, Roger, Marsada, and Daphne. As soon as they ate from a tray, Jamal requested that another tray be delivered.

"That's enough, I don't need anymore," said Marsada.

"Stop lying! You mean to tell me that you're satisfied and don't want anymore!" Jamal yelled as everyone laughed. Thanks to the waiters, Jamal's co-workers understood his point about contentment and the greater table that God has already prepared for His children.

Jamal believes that he has already won the lottery. Do you?

CROSS EXAMINATION – *Examined by the Cross*

1. *Is it possible to be in a position in which you have no wants? There is a difference between being content with what you have and having no wants. Is it possible to be completely filled while on earth?*
2. *Has God ever taken you to a place where you had no wants?*
3. *Does this place require wealth?*

"Ask God for His guidance; once you get the nod of God on your decisions, everything else will fall into place."
Jentezen Franklin

Day 48

Thy Kingdom Came?
Thy Kingdom Come?
Thy Kingdom Will Come?

"I am still confident of this:
I will see the goodness of the LORD in the land of the living.
Wait for the LORD; be strong and
take heart and wait for the LORD."
Psalm 27:13-14 - NIV

Connor screamed excitedly as he parked his car in front of the courthouse. "Thank you so much! You can't believe how much this call has made my day. My client will be ecstatic!" exulted the insurance defense attorney as he thanked Liza Motten, the county school superintendent, on his hands free mobile phone call.

"No, I'm just sorry to put you in this position. We should have gotten the documents you requested sooner. I don't know how we lost your subpoena," Liza apologized.

Walter Burkhouse, a history teacher, sued St. Stephen's Medical Center after a slip and fall in his hospital room. He claimed that he suffered severe headaches and memory loss because of the nursing staff's negligence.

As counsel for the hospital's insurance company, Connor tried to subpoena Walter's medical records to show that Walter had suffered strokes previously and had a history of headaches, memory loss, and losing his balance. Unfortunately, the court quashed the subpoena on the grounds that it would violate Mr. Burkhouse's privacy rights.

Connor subpoenaed the local school system for Mr. Burkhouse's personnel profile hoping to find records of his sick leave and any documentation indicating a history of headaches, memory loss, and vertigo well before his fall at the hospital. Mr. Burkhouse had no privacy rights in his employment records since he had sued for loss wages. Liza Motten, the Custodian of Records for the Smythe County Public School Systems now offered to send the documents within minutes of trial.

Connor thanked Liza for emailing Walter Burkhouse's personnel file. Within seconds, Connor paid for parking and flashed his bar badge to the security guards at the entrance metal detectors. The bar badge allowed him to bypass a security check and saved him a few minutes, but Connor still needed to jog to the law library to print the emailed records.

Four people typed on the four computer terminals in the library. Connor's heart sunk as his mobile phone revealed that he only had five minutes until trial. With his eyes closed, Connor prayed for help. He asked the Lord to open a computer terminal. It was highly unlikely that the judge would grant him a recess to print the files, so he needed the Red Sea that stood before him to somehow part.

"Excuse me, sir. Are you a lawyer?" asked a stranger in the library. Connor was slightly annoyed that his prayer had been interrupted and even more peeved about having to engage in a conversation that would eat up his remaining minutes before trial. He pulled his stress together and reasoned that he needed to see how this man may need legal advice.

"Yes, I am," Connor smiled a forced grin.

"Then, you don't have to wait for a computer. If you go through those doors, you will see the attorneys' lounge. Just show them your bar card and they'll let you in," the man offered. The man wore a badge that said "librarian." Connor thanked him and raced towards the lounge. He printed the personnel files and proceeded to victory at trial.

Critics often lament Christianity as a "pie in the sky" religion that is used to subjugate the masses. The word of God lays promises of *future* rewards in the kingdom for the sufferings of today; however, Christians, just like Connor, have a pass that provides access to the kingdom *right now* and while on earth. Connor missed out on the attorneys' lounge for years. Imagine all of the benefits of the kingdom that are accessible, yet missed by so many Christians.

Christians do not have to wait until death to enter the kingdom of God. Jesus states in Luke 17:21 that the "kingdom of God is within us." By accepting Jesus and allowing God to dwell within our hearts, the children of God declare their citizenship in heaven and celebrate the kingdom. One day, evil will be completely purged. One day, sin, hatred, and war, will be no more. One day, the invisible things of God will be made visible.

Until that day, God has given His people all power to overcome evil provided they walk in faith and use their pass to the throne of heaven. The Kingdom *came through* the cross. The Kingdom also *comes through* the infilling of the Holy Spirit. The Kingdom *will come* on earth as it is in heaven when our Savior returns.

Thank you, Lord for revealing your kingdom in so many ways. Through the cross, through the Holy Spirit, and through the return of our soon coming King. Let Thy Kingdom come in us and through us!

CROSS EXAMINATION – *Examined by the Cross*

Fortunately, the law librarian told Connor about the attorneys' lounge. Now imagine that someone greater than the librarian told you that you have the power to save souls, the power to heal people, the power to teach, the power to preach, the power to prophecy, or the power to do some other great work as a card carrying Christian. How would that change your life? How would it change the lives of the people around you? You have that pass! You have the kingdom inside of you!

"Christians display to us their wonderful
and confessedly striking method of life. . .
Every foreign land is to them as home,
yet their every homeland is foreign.
They pass their days on earth, but they are citizens of heaven.
They obey the laws of the land,
and at the same time surpass the law by their lives.
They love all and are reviled by all."

Anonymous Roman citizen
regarding first century Christians

By Gregory D. Yancey, Esq.

† ribulation

r eveals

i ntegrity

a nd

L ord's

S trengthening

CHAPTER 5

TRIALS OF THE BEATITUDES

"But He said,
'On the contrary, blessed are those who hear
the word of God and observe it."
Luke 11:28 - NASB

Day 49

Poor In Spirit, But Rich In Christ

"Blessed are the poor in spirit for
theirs is the kingdom of heaven."
Matthew 5:3 - NIV

Chad Kotier sighed with great relief as he entered the courtroom. He represented Officer Hemisi Adigwe in a shooting case. Dispatch sent Officer Adigwe to a house party for a disturbing the peace complaint. Upon his arrival, the home owner, Macy Ellington, yelled racial epithets to the African American officer as he walked along her sidewalk. Mary opened her front door and commanded her 110 pound pitbull to attack the officer.

In one fluid motion, Adigwe pulled out his service firearm and shot the dog. Officer Adigwe immediately requested backup to contain Macy Ellington and her hostile party guests. The Ellingtons later filed a multi-million dollar lawsuit against the city for negligence and destruction of property. To the city's embarrassment, the Ellington's address technically fell within the county and outside of the police department's jurisdiction. One side of the street fell in the city and the other side fell into the county even though the entire street had the same zip code.

Macy agreed to settle for one thousand dollars after Chad found a witness to corroborate the fact that she and her friends had been laughing and yelling epithets at the officer when she unleashed the dog.

After the settlement had been entered into the record, both attorneys approached the jurors to thank them for their time and to see how they would have decided the case. Attorneys often take this time to gain feedback on their presentation and to learn how jurors perceive evidence.

"I would've given her millions. I hate cops," said Juror 2.

"The officer should've used mace or his baton," reasoned Juror 3 before admitting that he would've used a gun against a charging pitbull.

"The guy is African, right? They're use to outrunning lions! He could have run from a dog," said Juror 7.

"The police department must have insurance for these things. They should just pay it. If they don't have insurance, they should at least have a big account of money from taxpayers for these things," concluded Juror 1.

Chad shook his head after he began to lose faith in the jury system. None of the jurors grasped the important issues of the case. They had allowed their own biases and prejudices to cloud their ability to analyze the evidence within the scope of the law.

"The cop was in the wrong neighborhood. They have to be held to a higher standard. I don't care if they are in hot pursuit of a murderer. . . if they ain't county cops . . .it ain't their business," said Juror 8.

Chad saw other jurors nodding in agreement. All of the Jurors except Juror 5 held deep resentment towards his client. Juror 5 brought him much needed encouragement.

"You did a great job. I mean. . . well, it wasn't just you. I mean God spoke through you very powerfully," said Juror 5.

"What do you mean?" Chad asked completely puzzled.

"Oops, you are a Christian, right?" asked Juror 5.

"Yes, but how did you know?" asked Chad.

"You were very humble and respectful to the judge unlike the other lawyer and Macy Ellington. You used words like grace. . . blessed . . .I don't know. . .you just sounded like a Christian. You were honest. You corrected things that you said when you believed you overstated something. I believe you really meant it when you thanked the jury for their service," added Juror 5.

Despite the disappointing comments that the other jurors had expressed, Chad felt good about himself knowing that he had honored God throughout the trial. Juror 5 encouraged Chad by telling him that he handled his job correctly while walking as a man who is poor in spirit. Chad never fully understood the meaning of this term until he met Juror 5.

The *poor in spirit* recognize that they need God for their daily bread and their daily strength. The *poor in spirit* walk humbly and find no pride in accomplishments or earthly possessions. The *poor in spirit* appreciate opportunities to serve the Lord and others without shame. The *poor in spirit* inherit the kingdom. Chad's behavior showed that he had the kingdom within him and that he was an heir to the throne. Juror 5 also carried herself as someone who was poor in spirit. While the other jurors sought to elevate themselves, Juror 5 exulted Chad. Blessed are the poor in spirit!

CROSS EXAMINATION - *Examined by the Cross*

1. *What does it mean to you to be poor in spirit? Why are the poor in spirit blessed? Why did Jesus refer to the poor in spirit in the first beatitude?*
2. *Have you ever been blessed by someone who was poor in spirit? What blessings have you received?*

"Poverty is freedom.
It is a freedom so that what I possess doesn't own me,
so that what I possess doesn't hold me down,
so that my possessions don't keep me from sharing
or giving of myself.
Rigorous poverty is our safeguard."

Mother Teresa

Day 50

BLESSED MOURNER

**"Blessed *are* they that mourn:
for they shall be comforted."
Matthew 5:4 - KJV**

This was one of those times which Todd hated having that analytical mind shared by lawyers. Why couldn't he just enjoy the eulogy instead of critiquing it in his head? The priest said, "Blessed are those who mourn." This contradiction only brought him agony instead of comfort. It was insulting. It sounded like one of those overused clichés like "God works in mysterious ways." Todd found no blessing after learning that his good friend and client, Harold, had been gunned down for the contents of his barbershop cash register. What possible blessing did Harold's widow or three young children derive from this tragedy?

Todd remembered helping Harold to incorporate his barbershop. Harold's magnetic personality instantly drew them to become friends.

A tear trickled from the attorney's eyes as he listened to the priest's reflection on Harold's tendency to quote scripture and to openly pray for people in his shop.

After the priest concluded his eulogy and closed the service with a prayer, people headed to Harold's widow, Renee, to pay respects. Todd had no idea what he would say to Renee or her children to comfort them. He found no "blessing" in his mourning and could see none in her grief.

"Renee, I'm so sorry for your loss. Harold was such a . . ." started Todd awkwardly before being interrupted.

"Did you see it? Did you notice it?" giggled Renee in the midst of teary eyes. After blowing her nose, she talked about the awesome wonder during the service. "Every time the priest said Harold's name, did you notice how the sun shined even more brightly through the stained glass?"

Todd started to feel the hairs on his arm raise from the goose bumps. She was right, in fact the sun shined again after she said Harold's name.

"In the past week, I've had a first row seat to countless miracles. I have never felt God's presence so clearly and tangibly. I feel Him weeping with me now. I felt that Harold was going to die that night, so I called him to tell him how much I loved him. He had been diagnosed with cancer months ago and perhaps the shooting saved him an agonizing battle," hypothesized Renee.

As the two talked, Todd realized the blessing in mourning. He could see God's love more clearly and he could feel God's comfort more profoundly. The clichés no longer felt like clichés, but pearls of wisdom.

CROSS EXAMINATION – *Examined by the Cross*

1. *Scripture says that mourners are blessed because they shall be comforted. Would they be better off not having to mourn in the first place?*
2. *What blessing have you found in mourning? What comfort have you received directly from the hand of God?*
3. *Are mourners actually blessed or do you believe people search for silver linings to comfort themselves?*
4. *Is Jesus referring solely to mourning the dead or is He also talking about godly sorrow about other things like injustice and sin? See 2 Corinthians 7:10.*

Day 51

No Weakness In Meekness

"Blessed *are* the meek:
for they shall inherit the earth."
Matthew 5:5 - KJV

Jelena arrived at the courthouse two hours before the doors opened just to stand near the front of the line. News vans from local and national stations lined up in expectation of the Anita Henison "murder trial of the century." The first year law student took a day off from classes to sit in on a once-in-a lifetime lesson. In addition to having an intellectual fascination about the model accused of killing her agent, Jelena deemed this to be an incredible classroom for good oral advocacy. The Anita Henison defense team comprised of three renowned battle-tested attorneys.

"Mavis Hornig, at the Goseppe Courthouse in downtown Carrysville. . ." said one reporter into a camera. Reporters talked and pontificated about the strategies of the prosecution and the defense. Occasionally, a reporter would interview a protester or bystander. The excitement only added to the weight of the wait.

The momentary relief of the opening of the courthouse doors soon dissipated as the metal detectors bottlenecked all entry into the building. Jelena only stood twenty feet away from the doorway when a huge gust of wind snatched papers out of the hands of the elderly woman in front of her. The gust scattered papers across the courtyard.

Although dreading to lose her spot, Jelena instinctively found herself chasing papers along the sidewalk as the elderly woman lost even more papers. No one else in line seemed interested in helping; in fact, the people who stood behind Jelena quickly closed in on her place in line. Exhausted, Jelena handed a stack of wrinkled sheets to their owner and apologized to the senior citizen for failing to gather all of the papers.

The law student made no attempt to reclaim her place in line out of fear of drawing the perception of cutting in front of people. Saddened, Jelena walked to the back of the line knowing that there was no chance that she would be able to see the "murder trial of the century."

"Young lady, where are you going?" inquired a security guard who now stood next to the elderly woman. "Didn't you come to see the Henison trial?" inquired another guard. To Jelena's surprise, the elderly woman turned out to be Judge Weslo's assistant, Eileen Franco.

Ms. Franco had forgotten her badge that day and waited in line. The security guards witnessed Jelena's kind act and led her ahead of the others into the courthouse and then into Judge Weslo's chambers. Not only did Jelena get to see the "trial of the century," she earned a clerkship with the judge who heard the trial of the century.

Years later after becoming a judge, Jelena credited one act of meekness and humility as a key moment in her life. She often reflected upon the time that she ran around the courtyard to retrieve Ms. Franco's papers as if it were her job. Meek people see themselves as servants to others, so they assume more responsibilities. At one bar event, Jelena said "Do not imitate the pomposity and arrogance that has tainted our profession. God rewards meekness and He promises that we will inherit the earth. Blessed are the meek!"

CROSS EXAMINATION – *Examined by the Cross*

1. *Have you ever been rewarded for an act of humility?*
2. *Have you ever felt greater by making yourself lower?*
3. *What does it mean to inherit the earth?*
4. *Do you believe that the meek will inherit the earth?*

Day 52

hUNGRY AND BLESSED

**"Blessed *are* they which do hunger and
thirst after righteousness:
for they shall be filled."
Matthew 5:6 - KJV**

"**A**re you okay?" texted Wendy. Tate felt ashamed as
he looked at the time on his phone. It was two o'clock in the
morning and he was still working in the office on the
Gundersen case. Once again, he probably needlessly worried
his wife. With trial only seven hours away, he had enough
time to take a power nap, shower, and to copy a few exhibits.
He had gone through this regimen so many times before that
he had become an expert at trying cases on minimum sleep.

Tate knew his client, Nathaniel Gundersen, had been a
trouble maker in the past; however, something jarred him
when Nathaniel expressed his gratitude for finding a job
through the Second Chance Employment Program ("SCEP").
Nathaniel, a reformed criminal, enjoyed working at the docks
where he unloaded luxury vehicles onto the pier. Prior to
SCEP, he had spent over a year trying to find work. Tate
refused to believe that Nathaniel would waste this
opportunity to steal cars. The trial lawyer did not believe the
allegations in the Statement of Charges.

Tate represented Nathaniel in a prior petty theft case and was broken hearted over the possibility that Nathaniel could have graduated to grand larceny. "How could Nate have broken into the warehouse and unloaded five Mercedes over a one month period? Why would he do something like that?" Tate pondered.

Tate spent hours looking through inventory records that he subpoenaed. The decreasingly optimistic defense attorney only wanted to learn the truth of what happened even if it meant his client's guilt. Tate also spent hundreds of his own dollars to obtain background records of the managers of the Pier Ten Merchants' Union. As he took one last look through the files, Tate noticed a discrepancy between the insurance claim and the police report. The insurance claim stated that ten cars were stolen; whereas, the police report only listed five. A quick search into neighboring state court records revealed that Nathaniel's employer reported many thefts and filed numerous claims against other insurance companies.

Tate deduced that someone in upper management fenced the cars that they stole and then benefitted from their insurance claims as well. After a long hot shower, a longer apology to his wife, and a short conversation with the State's Attorney, the charges were dismissed.

Tate's thirst for righteousness revealed a national scam in which the merchant union framed former felons in Second Chance Employment Program for thefts from the company.

CROSS EXAMINATION – *Examined by the Cross*

1. *How thirsty are you for righteousness – in yourself, in others, and in your community?*
2. *God quenched Tate's thirst for righteousness. Has he quenched yours?*
3. *How thirsty have you been? Have you lost sleep over it?*
4. *What is the blessing in being thirsty for righteousness?*
5. *Is your thirst for righteousness greater than your fear of others?*

"I lived every day with the threat of death
and I came to see many years ago that
I couldn't function if I allowed fear to overcome me.
The main thing is not how long I live,
but how well I have acquitted myself in the discharge
of these truths that are high, noble, and good."
Rev. Dr. Martin Luther King, Jr.

Day 53

Cycle of Mercy

**"Blessed *are* the merciful:
for they shall obtain mercy."
Matthew 5:7 - KJV**

"Jessica, I don't know what happened. We filed our complaint over two months ago and the court still hasn't issued a summons," explained Glen Hortnett. A few months ago, Jessica and Glen failed to resolve a personal injury claim between their clients so Glen filed a lawsuit. Jessica knew the court system in the city was overwhelmed and notoriously slow. She figured that it would take an additional month for the summons to be issued and then Glen would have to go through the task of trying to track down her client to serve him. Glen, a corporate attorney, had no real trial experience.

"Glen, don't sweat it. Email me a copy of the complaint. I will file a response on behalf of my client so we can speed things up. I'll also walk a copy of your complaint to the clerk. Terry probably misplaced it. They are short staffed due to the furlough," Jessica explained.

Glen sighed with much relief. His client had questioned his competency and threatened to fire his firm since months had passed without a court date. Jessica spared him two to three months of further stagnation and delay.

Three months later, Jessica emailed discovery requests to Glen asking for all evidence and witnesses that he intended to present at trial. Jessica, then, left a message on Glen's voicemail apologizing for sending late discovery. According to the rules of state civil procedure, Glen could refuse to produce discovery because of the missed deadline and refuse to disclose his witnesses and evidence. This would cause Jessica a substantial amount of embarrassment in front of her client and the judge.

For a moment, Glen entertained the idea of having a clear advantage in court over Jessica; however, he could not forget the mercy that she had shown him by accepting service of the complaint. Glen remembered that Jessica had even filed another copy of his complaint with the court. Glen could not forget the mercy that God and Jessica had shown him in covering up so many of his mistakes in this case, so it was imperative that he also show mercy as well. Glen accepted the discovery documents and provided complete answers and sets of documents to his colleague.

Jessica received mercy because she had been merciful.

CROSS EXAMINATION – *Examined by the Cross*

1. *Have you been merciful?*
2. *Do you see much mercy in the legal system?*
3. *Do you see mercy in your co-workers?*
4. *Some people say, "Let every beatitude be your attitude" but do you find any good in being merciful to unmerciful people?*
5. *Do you feel any difference in your relationship with God when you are merciful to others?*
6. *See Exodus 26:34, Exodus 30:6, and Numbers 7:89 regarding the positioning of the mercy seat above the ark of the testimony. What do you think of the quote below?*

"Notice that the mercy seat is placed over the law.
This tells us that God's mercy triumphs over judgment!"
Joseph Prince

Day 54

Pure Eyes to See The Pure God

"Blessed *are* the pure in heart:
for they shall see God."
Matthew 5:8 - KJV

E ver since she fell behind in billable hours, Katy avoided taking long lunch breaks. She had turned Nadine, a fellow associate and friend, down so many times that she could not decline another lunch invitation on one Thursday afternoon. The two associates had started with the firm at the same time and bonded through several trials by fires. Nadine had excelled in billable hours and made great strides down the partner track while Katy stumbled along. They were second year associates and Marquis, a new first year associate, had already surpassed Katy in monthly billable hours, expertise, and dependability.

"You know they'll be bringing in new associates next summer and they tend to release older associates who aren't firing on all cylinders," warned Nadine as the two stared at a homeless man shooing birds away from a trashcan.

"Thanks a lot! I was trying to avoid that, but you wanted to have lunch," Katy huffed. Nadine laughed at the homeless man as he fought the birds for a box of half eaten fried chicken. Katy found nothing funny about the scene.

"Just FYI, I'm first chair on a case with Marquis as my second chair. He was supposed to supervise the paralegals and collate all of the exhibits. I noticed one photograph missing which is essential to our case," whispered Nadine as if someone from the firm could possibly hear her devilish scheme.

Instead of correcting the mistake, Nadine decided to throw the case. She would later chew Marquis out in front of the client for not having the necessary exhibit. Nadine would then meet with the partners and the client to reimburse all damages sustained. "They would have to fire Marquis, " Nadine laughed. The homeless man stared at Katy and shook his head with disapproval.

Katy was sick to her stomach that Nadine would cause a nice guy his job and intentionally lose a case. Nadine explained to her that this was a dog eat dog world and that there was no way the partners will keep Marquis and Katy after the summer. As Nadine discussed the scheme, the homeless man sat between them on the bench.

"Watch this" yelled the homeless man as he tore a piece of breaded fried chicken into several tiny pieces and threw them to the ground. Crows throughout the park immediately descended on the discarded fast food. The homeless man grinned and told them that the crows were true bird brains.

"Don't they know that they are eating another bird? What kind of animal would eat its brother?" puzzled the homeless man with a wink to Katy.

"They're bird brains? They're eating the same thing you're eating, grandpa!" snapped Nadine.

"Sir, God has truly spoken through you to bless me. I have work to do, please take my lunch," smiled Katy as she headed back to the office. The second year associate refused to live without ethics or to be a dog in a dog eat dog world. Except for that one lunch break, Katy never encountered that homeless man again. She remembered the manner in which he smiled and had winked at her to drive home the importance of having integrity.

By being pure in heart, she saw God.

<u>CROSS EXAMINATION</u> – *Examined by the Cross*

1. *How do you define purity?*
2. *Is purity valued in your workplace?*
3. *Are you pure in heart? How do you obtain or maintain purity?*
4. *Why do you have to be pure in heart in order to see God?*
5. *Do you see God in your workplace?*
6. *Do people see God in you?*

"Our whole business in this life
is to restore to health the eyes of the heart,
whereby God may be seen."
St. Augustine

Day 55

BLESSED PEACE

**"Blessed *are* the peacemakers:
for they shall be called the children of God."
Matthew 5:9 - NIV**

Linda dropped a tattered greeting card on the table in front of her make shift moving crew. Her family and friends ate pizza around the conference room table as their muscles recovered from the long day of moving files and furniture to her new office.

"This is a big part of the reason why I'm moving my office. I received this card in the mail from my client's ex-wife after a divorce proceeding," Linda began as people wondered if their break was about to end. The crew quickly became intrigued as the attorney described the day his client dropped off scandalous photographs, emails, and text messages of his wife's elicit affairs.

"Guess what? I never used the evidence; in fact, I never mentioned to Mrs. Hollingsworth that I even had that stuff," Linda laughed. She simply called Mrs. Hollingsworth and asked her if she saw any way that the marriage could be reconciled and if she had considered marital counseling.

Mrs. Hollingsworth expressed great shame and remorse for the manner in which she treated her husband, but maintained that her lack of self-esteem and sexual addiction made it impossible to maintain a marriage.

"Mrs. Hollingsworth later thanked me for the advice that I had given her of where to get counseling so that she could find internal peace. Mr. Hollingsworth later informed her that I refused to use the dirt against her and helped him to divorce her amicably for the sake of their children," Linda continued.

"So what does this have to do with you changing offices? You got a thank you card from someone who was supposed to be an enemy, I don't get it," inquired Dinah.

"Over the years, Mrs. Hollingsworth has referred so many clients to me that I have basically maintained a practice off of those clients and then the people that those clients referred to me too," concluded Linda.

Lawyers have a unique opportunity to save the day for their clients. People call for counsel after a death, when a marriage dissolves, when a partnership breaks up, when bankruptcy seems unavoidable, and during many other uncertain life endeavors and crossroads. In no circumstance, do lawyers have a greater opportunity to display the character of the Savior than when they become peacemakers.

The Prince of Peace reconciled humanity with the Father, Jews with Gentiles, and even destroyed the barrier between clergy and laity. Blessed are the peacemakers because they follow in His steps!

CROSS EXAMINATION – *Examined by the Cross*

1. *This beatitude says that peacemakers will be called "children of God." Who will call you this?*
2. *Why does God value peacemakers? What does God think about people who incite dissension?*
3. *Describe an experience in which you have been a peacemaker.*
4. *Identify how you intend to be a peacemaker going forward.*

By Gregory D. Yancey, Esq.

Day 56

Goð Sees All

**"Blessed are those who are persecuted
because of righteousness,
for theirs is the kingdom of heaven."
Matthew 5:10 - NIV**

"Wayna, can you tell us any reason why Judge Harbaugh would file an Attorney Grievance complaint against you?" asked Evan Strahan. The lump in Wayna Coley's throat now traveled all the way down into her stomach. The litigator wanted to vomit. Wayna assumed that the partner called her to the office to assign her a new case or to negotiate an overdue salary increase. She had no idea that Judge Harbaugh had filed a complaint against her. She found it equally puzzling that the partners learned this information before her. The Attorney Grievance Commission upholds the confidentiality of these complaints, yet the partners had a copy. Wayna concluded that Judge Harbaugh had sent them a copy of his grievance letter to get her fired.

"Judge Harbaugh sets bail much higher than any other judge in the courthouse. I told him that he violated the 8th Amendment's prohibition against cruel and unusual punishment after he set a $200,000 bail for a simple assault case for a first time offender. There were no medical injuries and the case boiled down to his word versus her word," Wayna maintained. Even if found guilty, the client faced no real jail time.

Wayna explained as she divulged her beliefs of judicial corruption. Bail bondsmen financed Judge Harbaugh's election campaign. The same bondsmen who contributed to his campaigns were permitted to sit in his courtroom and to pass out their business cards in the hallways after bail reviews.

"This is a conflict of interest. He's setting high bail for poor people facing minor charges," preached Wayna.

"Judge Harbaugh claims that you were unprepared in court and could not cite statutory justifications for reduced bail," interrupted Jennifer Strahan, Evan Strahan's partner in Strahan & Strahan as well as in marriage.

"I cited statutes and common law, but this is also common sense. It's an issue of ethics. He is requiring first time offenders to come up with twenty thousand dollars just to prove their innocence. That's worse than the punishment they would get if proven guilty. We're talking first time offenders who will get probation!" screamed Wayna.

The partners did not want to hear anymore. As longtime associates of Judge Harbaugh, the partners fully understood the corrupt bond setting practices. They benefitted from many of his rulings even when the facts and the law stood against them. Wayna angered a true ally of the firm. In addition to having to defend a complaint with the Attorney Grievance Commission, she would have to find a new job. They fired her for no other reason than for telling the truth. In their way of life, her honesty made her evil.

Strahan & Strahan persecuted Wayna for being righteous. The word of God tells us that Wayna has the kingdom of heaven even though she lost a court hearing, lost her job, and lost money to hire legal representation to fight a frivolous Attorney Grievance Commission complaint.

Jesus says that the kingdom of heaven is inside of the believer. Not only does the kingdom provide peace and guidance, but it also stirs dissension and persecution from those who do not belong to it. The persecutors of the righteous will receive their dues. Do not get upset when the wicked seem to prosper. Always remember that:

God sees all and one day all will see God.

Cross Examination – *Examined by the Cross*

1. *Have you ever been persecuted for doing something righteous?*
2. *What were the circumstances?*
3. *How did you handle it?*
4. *See Acts 5:41 – Why would the apostles rejoice after suffering persecution?*

"If you are poor in spirit, His kingdom He gives you. If you mourn, comfort He offers you. If you are meek, inheritance He leaves you. If you hunger and thirst for righteousness,
He will fill you.
If you're merciful, mercy He gives you.
If you're pure in heart, His face He shows you.
If you're a peacemaker, His son He names you. . ."
Hazem Farraj

Day 57

Blessed Insults

**"Blessed are you when people insult you,
persecute you and falsely say all kinds of evil
against you because of me."
Matthew 5:11 - NIV**

"They suspended me just because I told an atheist student that intelligent people can have different beliefs. I wasn't preaching or proselytizing. I didn't even discuss my beliefs," explained Dr. Portia Mileva the embattled philosophy professor.

"Yeah, but you're a ministry leader at some church and you've published articles about your faith. I've been around for decades without making waves. You won't last here long," rebutted Ivan Rakin, the campus Equal Employment Opportunity Commission ("EEOC") representative. The Board knew that Dr. Mileva only discussed her beliefs when cornered, yet wanted to sanction her for discussing them at all. The Board temporarily suspended her before as a warning to avoid any "extracurricular" statements of faith that could be attributed to the university. Now, Dr. Mileva faced the prospect of unemployment once again. Students called her "Professor Piety" and "Dr. Madonna," yet no one deemed that to be as offensive as her stating that she believed in the Bible.

Ivan Rakin, a retired practicing attorney, appreciated the benefits of having a cushy campus position as the EEOC attorney. Human Resources frequently sent disgruntled employees to him and he simply advised them not to make any waves. The EEOC attorney is supposed to be an advocate for faculty and staff against the administration when people are treated unfairly due to their race, gender, religion, and age, yet Ivan had no conviction.

He never filed complaints of discrimination regardless of the evidence or pattern of complaints raised by university staff. He discussed his history with the university as an example to Mileva. The EEOC attorney watched several different university presidents come and go throughout the years. Ivan outlasted various academic movements and seen leading professors fired, yet his position never came in jeopardy. He attended campus functions without ever running into an adversary, because he had no enemies. Ivan considered himself to be a peacemaker, when he was actually a conformist.

"But no one respects you. You're not serving the school or the staff. You're supposed to keep the administration accountable for discrimination. Just because you don't have enemies doesn't mean you're doing any good. As far as I'm concerned, you are godless," argued Mileva.

Ivan proved to be correct in that Mileva would not last there much longer. Within three weeks, the suspension became a termination. After termination, Mileva spent four months unemployed before discovering a professorship at a seminary.

Mileva's times of persecution produced a closeness to God that she had never known. She had heard about spiritual warfare, but now she had experienced it. Persecution made God and Satan more and more tangible as she developed the ability to see the divinity in her supporters and supernatural evil in her detractors. Mileva reasoned that every insult and slight in the midst of persecution provided a blessing after all.

Mileva had also been correct about Ivan. The "yes man" never made a difference at the university. His retirement party was as empty as his accomplishments. Ivan wished that someone at the party could have discussed at least one moment in which he had taken a stand for something or for some one. He had never been insulted or despised for standing for righteousness.

CROSS EXAMINATION – *Examined by the Cross*

1. Why does Jesus say that we are blessed when we are persecuted and insulted because of Him?
2. Have you ever been persecuted or insulted because of Him? If so, what happened? If not, does this mean that you aren't living for Him?
3. Some people are persecuted for being Christians and some are persecuted for being annoying self-righteous Pharisees. How do you tell the difference?

"Thus it begins; the cross is not the terrible end to an otherwise God-fearing and happy life, but it meets us at the beginning of our communion with Christ.
When Christ calls a man, he bids him come and die."
Dietrich Bonhoeffer

By Gregory D. Yancey, Esq.

† ribulation

r eveals

i ntegrity

a nd

L ord's

S trengthening

CHAPTER 6

TRIALS OF THE CROSS

"Then Jesus said to his disciples,
'If anyone would come after me,
he must deny himself
and take up his cross and follow me.'"
Matthew 16:24 NIV

Day 58

GOVERNMENT ON My Shoulders

**"For unto us a child is born, unto us a Son is given:
and the government shall be upon his shoulder:
and his name shall be Wonderful, Counseller[14],
The mighty God, The everlasting Father, The Prince of Peace."**
Isaiah 9:6 KJV

"Just keep in mind that people in the village where we are going do not have the freedoms that we have in our country. Take Catelyn here, she could be beheaded for wearing a crop top like that, or Bruce could be killed just for wearing his cross," Director Julio Vargas warned his volunteer attorney corps in their briefing. Many of the volunteer attorneys suddenly began to fully appreciate the danger within their trip to the African country.

The volunteers enlisted with the purpose to enter war torn territories, study the legal system of the previous administration, study the human rights violations suffered by refugees, and empower the people to develop laws and a legal system that would benefit all.

---

[14] This is the King James spelling for the word "counselors." The KJV also translates two separate names for Jesus: Wonderful and Counselor; whereas, the NIV identifies one name: Wonderful Counselor.

The volunteer corps would serve as an advisory board to the interim government as well as to the people. The inherent danger simmered within the militarized groups that did not welcome change.

"I don't understand how peacekeepers can be a threat," Bruce pondered aloud. He could not understand why someone would want to kill him for trying to make a system of due process. He could not understand how a cross could incite hatred.

"Did you hear about what happened over two thousand years ago? Herod massacred babies because of a prophecy about a Prince of Peace. You must have missed that day in history class," Julio joked sarcastically.

"Any illegitimate government is threatened by a system that allows people access to rightful rulers. Just as Satan's temporary government resists Jesus Christ and the people of God, the governments of this world will be on the shoulders of people who rise against it to assert their God given rights," interjected Chaplain Forsythe to explain the offensiveness of peace and the cross to oppressors.

People are often shocked, confused, and even disarmed by the enmity that the wicked have for the righteous. The injustice is greatly magnified when government leaders are the bad actors. Jesus endured his cross and triumphed through it. Christ followers will too.

CROSS EXAMINATION - *Examined by the Cross*

1. *Have you ever had an experience in which you felt the government on your shoulders? What happened?*
2. *Do you see the transitions in Isaiah 9:6 which state: 1) a Son is given, 2) the government would be on His shoulders, and 3) the Messiah would be called by various great names?*
3. *Why was the government on His shoulders?*
4. *Cite examples of governments which stand in opposition to peace today. Do you see examples in which some governments are opposing Christ?*
5. *How has Jesus conquered governments as the Wonderful Counselor*, the mighty God, the everlasting Father, and the Prince of Peace?*
6. *How will Jesus conquer the world systems in the end times?*

*NIV translation, but the KJV lists Wonderful and Counselor as two separate names.

Day 59

Shrewd as Snakes

"If the home is deserving, let your peace rest on it;
if it is not, let your peace return to you.
If anyone will not welcome you or listen to your words,
shake the dust off your feet
when you leave that home or town. . .
I am sending you out like sheep among wolves.
Therefore be as shrewd as snakes and
as innocent as doves."
Matthew 10:13-16 in part NIV

"We don't want an autopsy done for religious reasons. We don't believe in the desecration of the body," Jimbo Kincaid explained to Aaron Price.

Aaron never made house calls to potential clients; however, this case required discretion. The local news provided around the clock coverage of eleven year old Bethany Kincaid's death after a routine tonsillectomy. Aaron figured that he could gather more insight into the family and Bethany's background by visiting their home. He also found no need to be thrown into the media circus until he was 100% certain that he was taking the case.

"I believe the medical staff used the wrong kind of anesthesia or something. They must have used an adult dose on my child," offered Francine Kincaid, Jimbo's wife.

Aaron apologized for jumping right into his legal analysis and requested that everyone come together in prayer so that God may be in the midst of their conversation. Jimbo politely declined and explained that he was not a Christian, but respected the beliefs of others.

"Did that belong to Bethany?" asked Aaron noticing a small pink inhaler on the floor next to the coffee table.

Jimbo tried to change the subject before admitting that his daughter had respiratory problems. She had forgotten her inhaler the morning of her tonsillectomy and had started wheezing. The surgeons would not have performed the surgery if Bethany appeared sick. Francine could not afford to take off of work again. To avoid having to postpone the procedure, she broke her allergy relief pill in half and gave it to her daughter.

"We don't think the medicine caused her death. We know they'll try to put it on the medicine or Bethany's asthma if they do an autopsy. They could even try to charge us for murder or something. I know it was them doctors!" Francine yelled.

"Mr. and Mrs. Kincaid, an autopsy is the only way for us to know the truth. I only deal from the top of the deck. I'm not going to accuse a physician of causing a death if Bethany died from taking adult medication or going under anesthesia while having other respiratory problems," Aaron argued.

"I thought the client was supposed to be the boss. I guess we need a real lawyer who isn't too arrogant to listen," fired Jimbo along with a threat to kill Aaron if word ever got out about Bethany's asthma or use of adult sinus medication.

"Our conversation is confidential. I take my oath seriously. You'll find out soon enough that you don't want a dishonest lawyer. Dishonest lawyers are like snakes. They have a way of biting everyone," Aaron concluded as he put on his coat and left the home.

The embattled attorney wiped his hands as if saying that he wiped his hands clean of the case. Once outside, he wiped his feet on the doormat to shake off the dust as Jesus advised in Matthew 10:13-16. The Kincaids sought to sue the hospital for giving their daughter an adult dose of anesthesia when they had given the child an adult dose of medication. They probably caused a death, yet seek to sue the hospital. Aaron praised God for revealing the Kincaids' true character. The people of God must know the ways of the snake without becoming one.

CROSS EXAMINATION – *Examined by the Cross*

1. Have you accepted the fact that some people will not receive your advice?
2. How does it feel to know that Jesus gives you permission to shake the dust off your feet and to leave unreceptive people?
3. How does it feel to know that Jesus advises us to be as shrewd as snakes but innocent as doves in this world?
4. Every lawyer is tempted not only to eat forbidden fruit, but to become the snake. Have you ever been tempted to be a snake?
5. Aaron rejected a case that could have given him fortune and fame, what have you turned down in order to stay righteous?

"Deception is Satan's number one weapon,
and discernment is our number one defense."
Jentezen Franklin

Day 60

Forcefully Advancing

**"From the days of John the Baptist until now,
the kingdom of heaven has been forcefully advancing,
and forceful men lay hold of it."
Matthew 11:12 - NIV**

"I want you to look the judge in the eyes tomorrow and demand that Mr. Kournapple compensate you for back pay and for all the mental anguish that he has caused you and your family as a result of the sexual harassment. Do not *ask* the judge, *demand* to be made whole!" Jacinta advised as she shook her client, Belania's, hand one last time in the lobby of the firm. Jacinta felt good about the trial preparation session that she conducted with the assistance of her law clerk, Tina.

"Don't you think that was a little strong? I thought lawyers weren't supposed to coach clients about testifying. Are you sure you want her demanding anything from a judge?" Tina inquired.

"We're going before Judge Cranton. He is extremely laid back and pro-Defendant. One thing about Cranton is that he responds to emotion. If you don't care, then he doesn't care. He'll sleep during a trial if you let him," Jacinta explained.

Jacinta respected Tina's question and enjoyed teaching opportunities. "In court, we have the burden to change the status quo. We have the burden to convince the judge to punish a company and to require them to pay our client. You cannot change the status quo by being passive. You cannot change the status quo by simply presenting facts and hoping that people will differentiate right from wrong. You change the status quo by being forceful," Jacinta explained.

The experienced trial attorney clarified her remarks by stating that a party should never be disrespectful, loud, or even violent in court; however, a plaintiff cannot get change without being assertive, confident, and prepared. Jacinta did not coach her client to lie, but to be assertive, confident, and prepared.

No attorney wants to pull teeth to get a client to express a complaint at trial. In court, Belania required no follow up questions about her suffering. She looked the judge in the eyes, testified clearly about Mr. Kournapple's sexual harassment, and demanded that he be brought to justice. Judge Cranton responded to Belania's boldness with a hefty verdict in her favor.

Scripture reminds us to be bold before the throne of God and that we must be bold before men as well.

CROSS EXAMINATION – *Examined by the Cross*

1. *Did you know that the kingdom of heaven is forcefully advancing?*
2. *In what ways were Jesus and John the Baptist forceful men?*
3. *Have you staked your claim to the kingdom?*
4. *Are you a forceful man or woman?*
5. *How have you affected the status quo for the kingdom?*
6. *What does it mean to go boldly before the throne in Hebrews 4:16 KJV?*
7. *Do you show passion when making your requests to your Heavenly Father?*
8. *Do you show passion when making a plea for justice to others?*
9. *In which areas of your life do you need more boldness?*

"My thoughts are guided by God's Word every day. No obstacle can defeat me, because my mind is programmed for victory. This is my declaration."
Joel Osteen

Day 61

GIVING TO CAESAR

"They came to him and said, 'Teacher, we know that you are a man of
integrity. . .Is it right to pay taxes to Caesar or not?
Should we pay or shouldn't we?'
But Jesus knew their hypocrisy.
'Why are you trying to trap me?' he asked.
'Bring me a denarius and let me look at it.'
They brought the coin, and he asked them,
'Whose portrait is this? And whose inscription?'
'Caesar's,' they replied.
Then Jesus said to them, 'Give to Caesar what is Caesar's and
to God what is God's.'
And they were amazed at him."
Mark 12:14-17 in part - NIV

"Thanks Sienna, for agreeing to take my case on such
short notice. I've been going through some tough times. . .
well. . .. um. . . moneywise lately. That's why my tags were
expired when the cop pulled me over. I didn't want to give
you a check and take a chance on it not clearing," Dedrick
explained as he handed counsel an envelope with one
thousand dollars in cash.

As Sienna walked her client out of the conference room
and into the lobby of her firm, she could not help but to think
of all the personal bills that she had to pay. One of the perks
of owning a law firm rested in the fact that she saw every
dollar that entered the firm and every dollar that left the firm.

Cash payments enabled her to pay personal bills, put gas in the car or even buy dinner without having a written record of income received.

Any recorded income only meant that she would increase her tax obligations. Sienna hated seeing money deducted from her paycheck for tax withholdings, payroll tax, unemployment insurance tax, and other taxes. The last three cash payments received never made it to the bank, so what was different about the Dedrick Pollard payment? Why did Sienna feel this unyielding guilt about using the money to pay her bills when she worked so hard? Was she feeling guilty merely because Dedrick went to her church? Sienna suddenly felt an overwhelming fear of disappointing God even though she had good intentions in how she would spend the money. She charged Dedrick, a brother from her church addiction recovery ministry, less than other attorneys and intended to use the money to pay creditors and tithes. If she withheld taxes, then she would lose almost a third of the money.

Sienna saw little likelihood that she would ever get caught for tax evasion; however, she felt as if she had already been caught. Somehow, she feared that her Christian witness had been compromised. Sienna knew that God was watching her and recalled the exchange between Jesus and the Pharisees in Mark 12:14-17.

Jesus submitted simultaneously to the Father and to government leaders. Sienna reasoned that she was required to submit to the government even while doing God's work. She took a quick glance at the faces and seals on the bills as she drove to the bank ATM and deposited the cash into her business bank account.

"I guess I'll give to Caesar what is his," Sienna said as she returned to the office to prep for the Pollard case. This meant that she would not be able to spend the money until payday and that she would have less money after withholding taxes, but her conscience was clear.

"I'm not going to fall into the trap. I'm not going to let the devil have anything over me," Sienna decided as she listened to music from her favorite gospel music radio station.

CROSS EXAMINATION - *Examined by the Cross*

1. *Jesus was crucified by a corrupted government, so why would He require us to pay taxes?*
2. *Why did Jesus view the question about paying taxes as a trap? Was it a trap for him to defy the government, a trap for ego and pride, or was it a trap to invite lust for money and wealth?*
3. *How can this be a trap for us if there is little likelihood of ever getting caught?*

Day 62

LOOSED ON EARTH

**"I tell you the truth, whatever you bind on earth
will be bound in heaven, and
whatever you loose on earth will be loosed in heaven."
Matthew 18:18 - NIV**

" I already discussed this with my client and he's okay with it. He feels badly about hurting his wife, but he doesn't love her anymore. He had to move on. He has apologized hundreds of times, but she can't hear it. Instead of having my client pay me another $20,000 in legal fees and causing Mrs. Taylor any more fees for a pointless trial, let's give her the vindication that she needs now," concluded Fernando Retuirrez as he watched the bewilderment of the learned judge and opposing counsel while in chambers.

"I don't know how you passed the bar. This is the craziest thing I have ever heard. You want me to call your client a scumbag in open court!" yelled Judge Kranville, the settlement judge. Judge Kranville and attorney, Ruwina Madison, stood in awe as Fernando Retuirrez explained his innovative solution to resolve the case.

"Mr. Taylor has already agreed to pay child support, alimony, and to even give his wife the marital home, but she still isn't satisfied. She's still hurt by the fact that he cheated and moved on with his life," argued Retuirrez.

Ruwina Madison could not deny this point. Her client was a wreck. She had seen multiple therapists and had been prescribed several medications to help her deal with the separation. Kendra Taylor had lost hair, weight, and it was only a matter of time before she lost her life – or would try to take it. The parties had nothing left to fight over, but Mrs. Taylor refused to agree to any terms of a divorce stating that she did not want "him to get off that easily." Retuirrez suggested that a formal reprimand of Mr. Taylor in open court would give her the justice that she needed.

"I guess if it'll clear a docket and if it'll get these people to move on with their lives. Mrs. Madison, I know you have issues with lying. Tell your client that she should accept the deal. Tell her that the judge who tries the case might not value marriage like I do and I want to tell Mr. Taylor how much of a dirt bag he is right now!" barked Judge Kranville.

"But, it's still lying. I'm sure you want me to leave out the part where Mr. Taylor *agreed* to be yelled at. This is a charade," said Ruwina as she reluctantly backed down. She had also grown tired of the case. She hated seeing her client self-destruct. The Taylors had been separated for three years and Mr. Taylor had already moved in with someone else. Mrs. Taylor had no expectation of reconciling; in fact, she only blocked the divorce to make Mr. Taylor suffer.

Reluctantly, Ruwina exited chambers and followed the judge's orders. Mrs. Taylor accepted the settlement terms after some prodding. Ruwina explained to Kendra that she needed to forgive Mr. Taylor for her own well-being and the well-being of the children.

Judge Kranville proceeded to tell Mr. Taylor that he forfeited his right to be called a man the day he cheated on his wife. "Married men do not leave their wife and children to go out on dates," Kranville yelled. Kendra Taylor cried loud sobs that could be heard from the hallway of the courtroom as Kranville tore into her soon-to-be ex-husband.

The reprimand was no longer a charade. Judge Kranville's anger reached new heights as he saw years of sacrifice, love, and commitment wash down the Plaintiff's face through tears. Retuirrez and Mr. Taylor were duly shamed for the agony that Kendra had suffered.

Kendra felt cleansed, relieved, and even a little pity for the "scumbag." There was a part of her that wanted revenge; however, she truly wanted an acknowledgement of her pain. Mr. Taylor's previous apologies had no meaning because she was not ready to forgive him and he did not seem to hurt as much as she had suffered. Kendra finally discovered that all the time that she spent binding him, she had bound herself. In the courtroom, she released everything. She released all anger, all fear, and all unforgiveness realizing that her resentment was only self-torture. She forgave Mr. Taylor for her own healing and trusted God for a better future. Ruwina rejoiced in her client's new freedom, but felt bounded by shame for being part of a lie.

CROSS EXAMINATION – *Examined by the Cross*

1. *In Matthew 18:18, Jesus declares that believers have the power to bind on earth and in heaven. What or whom did Kendra bind?*
2. *In Matthew 18:18, Jesus declares that believers have the power to loose on earth and in heaven. What or whom did Kendra loose?*
3. *What are the physical and spiritual ramifications of binding and loosing someone or something?*
4. *Who are you binding? Who are you loosing?*
5. *What should Ruwina do to feel loose and unbounded?*

Day 63

Do This For The Least of These

"The King will reply, 'I tell you the truth,, whatever you did for one of the least of these brothers of mine, you did for me.'"
Matthew 25:40 - NIV

Sidney Weiland volunteered to speak at the Meningdon Domestic Violence Shelter partially to help women in distress, but primarily to market his family law practice. He needed to bring in new clients and figured this to be a great way to do a good deed while letting people know about his law firm. He would only have to speak for thirty minutes about the process of filing for a protective order then he would hand out his business cards with the hopes of getting some divorce clients. Sidney also hoped to get a few photos with the staff and the domestic violence victims for his website and social media posts.

As the young attorney fielded question after question, he soon realized that the women lacked the financial means to ever hire him. Most of them fled their abusers and were clearly trying to rebuild their lives.

"If these people had money, they probably would've worked out their issues with private therapists instead of going to a shelter," Sidney thought as he wanted to kick himself for the fruitless marketing effort. He was tapped out on *pro bono* projects and needed billable hours for the firm to close out the quarter with respectable numbers.

While Sidney pondered the best way to wrap up the question and answer segment, Freda McIntosh entered the room and sat in the back corner with her arms wrapped around her knees. The seemingly strange woman pointed to Sidney several times as the staff workers asked, "Freda, do you want to talk to Mr. Weiland?" Freda nodded, but then hid her face behind her hands.

A staff member with the name tag "Nancy" explained that Freda had been imprisoned by her ex-husband for several years. She had been kept in a cage at times, beaten, burned, stabbed, choked, and raped. To this day, she suffers social phobias and anxiety disorders which cause her to have panic attacks whenever she is around men. Freda is still unable to do basic things such as grocery shop or go to any place where she may encounter a male.

Freda left her one-on-one counseling session and was drawn to Sidney's presentation. No one could have imagined that she would walk up to Sidney Weiland, a lawyer of all people, without having a panic attack. They figured that if Freda ever became comfortable around a male again it would be a therapist, a physician, or a pastor.

"Freda is taking paralegal classes online so she can eventually help other survivors of domestic violence. She's having some problems with civil procedure and unfortunately, none of us can provide much help," explained Nancy.

"My paralegal, Gina, and I would be happy to tutor her," said Sidney. He had initially hoped that speaking at the shelter would lead to a benefit and it produced one he never could have imagined. Sidney was honored to be part of Freda's courageous transformation from victim to victor. The family law attorney no longer had the desire to collect photos of victims for his website or social media posts, but a passion to be their advocate. His practice suddenly had meaning and significance as he represented more and more people like Freda. By doing for the "least of these," he ended up becoming a hand of God which touched so many lives.

CROSS EXAMINATION – *Examined by the Cross*

1. *How did Sidney serve the Lord by serving others?*
2. *When was the last time you served the Lord by serving others?*
3. *Even with the wrong motivation, Sidney had still provided a service for the "least of these." From God's perspective, what changes when we have the correct motivation?*
4. *Read the quote below. Charity becomes more meaningful when it comes at a cost. What costs are you willing to bear? Do you agree with the notion that a true servant must feel "oppression" in his/her soul to help others?*

"Whoever will become a preacher must feel the needs of men
until it becomes an oppression to his soul."
Leslie J. Tizard

Day 64

PERSISTENT PRAYER

Then Jesus told his disciples a parable to show them that they should always pray and not give up. He said: "In a certain town there was a judge who neither feared God nor cared about men. And there was a widow in that town who kept coming to him with the plea, 'Grant me justice against my adversary.'

"For some time he refused. But finally he said to himself, 'Even though I don't fear God or care about men, yet because this widow keeps bothering me, I will see that she gets justice, so that she won't eventually wear me out with her coming!'"

And the Lord said, "Listen to what the unjust judge says. And will not God bring about justice for his chosen ones, who cry out to him day and night? Will he keep putting them off? I tell you, he will see that they get justice, and quickly. However, when the Son of Man comes, will he find faith on the earth?"

Luke 18:1-8 - NIV

Tanille Sutton hated being buzzed by the receptionist when drafting a pleading. Her writing skills had diminished over the years as more and more of her cases settled out of court. She readily copied pleadings from other cases, but when she ventured into a different practice area the attorney needed total concentration.

"Ms. Henley wants to talk to you again," Chris chimed through the phone speaker with a chuckle. Tanille just met with Ms. Henley yesterday, yet this lady already started to pester her.

The prospective client clearly lacked the means to hire counsel. Even worse, she had already left two messages on Tanille's voicemail that morning. Tanille could not believe that she was considering taking this case especially for a client that would probably call so much.

"Please tell her that I'm busy and I . . . um never mind. I'll take the call," Tanille waffled. Ms. Henley quickly greeted Tanille and thanked her for taking the call. Within seconds, Ms. Henley told Tanille that she had been the answer to her prayers. Tanille shook her head and could not help but to laugh at the audacity of the elderly woman to believe that she could hire an attorney in her firm without having any money. Ms. Henley told several of her neighbors that she had a good Christian lawyer who would stand up for her against the car dealership even before their first meeting.

As Tanille drafted her pleadings, she wondered how this woman with little education and little financial resources had succeeded in getting her to take this case. "If I had half of her boldness, I would have gotten a raise by now," Tanille thought as she opened a file for her new client.

Lawyers must be persistent. So many in the legal profession get frustrated when a motion is denied, when a case is lost, when contract terms are rejected, or even when a name is slandered. However, Jesus commands the Church to be persistent in prayer to the Father and persistent in seeking justice.

The battle is not often won by strength, intelligence, influence, or clever words but through diligence. The parable of the persistent widow shows that an evil powerful judge, who had no fear of God or public perception, could only be moved by a person who refused to accept injustice. Unlike the wicked judge, God desires justice and He hurts from the cries of His children. The Lord promises justice to the persistent and exchanges miracles for faith.

Jesus poses a serious challenge to believers. He asks if he will find such "faith on the earth." Have you cried out day and night for justice? Have you asked others to join you in praying for change? Do you persistently pray for the sick? Do you stay on your knees for a clearer understanding of your purpose? Ms. Henley persistently cried out for justice until she found an advocate who would take her case. Have you cried out to your advocate in heaven with all of your strength? Have you asked Jesus to take your case?

Athletes say they want to leave everything on the field. They do not want to leave the arena without knowing they tried everything and fought with all of their strength. If you are not persistent in your prayers, then you have not fought injustice with all of your strength. Pray for justice without ceasing! Cry out to Him day and night! Be faithful! Be persistent!

CROSS EXAMINATION – *Examined by the Cross*

1. *Do you have a prayer journal to track your prayers and the Lord's answer?*
2. *Have you demonstrated the fervent prayer life of the persistent widow? When Jesus or the Holy Spirit comes will they find such faith in you?*
3. *Identify one prayer need and make it a point to go before the Lord daily for the next thirty days. Ask Him persistently in faith.*

"Prayer has brought hearing to the deaf, sight to the blind, life to the dead, salvation to the lost, and healing to the sick. Prevailing prayer should be the main business of our day."
Jentezen Franklin

Day 65

New and Old Treasures

"He said to them,
'Therefore every teacher of the law
who has been instructed about the kingdom of heaven
is like the owner of a house who brings out of his storeroom
new treasures as well as old."
Matthew 13:52 - NIV

Uche Adamante's estate easily valued over one hundred and fifty million dollars. Paula Fuentes enjoyed representing the renowned philanthropist for decades. In addition to preparing his will, she administered numerous charitable foundations, trusts, and scholarships for Mr. Adamante. Upon his death, Paula handled the probate and ensured that property items were disseminated in accordance to the will; however, Uche still had millions of dollars worth of personal property, art, and furniture within his mansion that had to be disposed. Uche's widow, Marcia Adamante, had no intention of remaining in their home in the Hamptons without her husband. She decided it was best to downsize and to move to California to live near her siblings. Marcia needed to get rid of much of the household items quickly.

Paula attended the estate sale to provide moral support to Marcia. The estate sale drew buyers from around the world primarily because of the memorabilia that Mr. Adamante acquired from encounters with various celebrities. On day three of the sale, Marcia and her daughters passed out fliers, made calls, and sent invitations through social media for anyone and everyone to come to their lawn to receive a free gift.

In true Adamante fashion, the family handed out valuable jewelry, authentic African sculptures, traditional dashikis and African garb, furniture, and other household items which remained unsold. The Adamantes gave away unused items as well as antique items that could have easily raised another two million dollars.

"This does not compare to the riches in Christ Jesus that my husband gave away," Marcia laughed as if she were a child. All of the children, except the youngest daughter, Sanaa, shared their mother's zeal and joy. Sanaa seemed quite saddened.

"What's the matter, Sanaa?" Paula asked expecting to hear the nine year old grieve for her father or grieve over the items given away.

"We made some people happy, but we could have made more people happy if more people came to the house. They didn't believe us. They didn't know what my father had. They didn't know what we were giving away," Sanaa grimaced. The girl marveled over the people who came to the house, but was saddened by the majority of the people who failed to accept their invitations.

Paula reflected upon Sanaa's grief and frustration. The attorney experienced similar grief and frustration when she invited family members to her church. At times, she felt like crying, "*They didn't believe us. They didn't know what my Father had. They didn't know what we were giving away.*"

Paula tried her best to share the treasures of the gospel with loved ones but they refused her each time. In Matthew 13:52, Jesus compares teachers of the gospel to a man who brings new and old treasures from a storeroom. The gospel contains new treasures because the word of God applies to circumstances that believers face daily. The gospel also contains old treasures and wisdom that is as timeless as our God.

Cʀᴏss Exᴀᴍɪɴᴀᴛɪᴏɴ - *Examined by the Cross*

1. *Do you know what the Father has in store for you?*
2. *Do you know what He is giving away?*
3. *Have you accepted these new and old treasures?*
4. *Do you know that as a teacher of the gospel, you are giving away items that are more valuable than Mr. Adamante's estate?*
5. *Are you giving away the new and old treasures in the gospel of Jesus Christ to others?*
6. *Read the exchange below. What treasure did August Spangenberg give to John Wesley?*

August Spangenberg: Do you know Jesus Christ?
John Wesley: I know He is the Savior of the world?
August Spangenberg: True, but do you know He has saved you?

Day 66

PATERNITY TESTED

**"As soon as Jesus was baptized,
he went up out of the water.
At that moment heaven was opened,
and he saw the Spirit of God descending like a dove
and lighting on him.
And a voice from heaven said,
'This is my son, whom I love;
with him I am well pleased."
Matthew 3:16-17 - NIV**

"The results of the test revealed that there is a 99.9% certainty that Dale Bronner is the biological father of Cody Felton," announced the court clerk.

"Hallelujah! Thank you, Jesus!!" Dale cried as his attorney smiled.

Judge Harriet Grayson stood in total disbelief. She had become accustomed to men denying paternity to avoid child support obligations, yet this individual rejoiced. Dale wanted to be in his son's life. Adalina Felton, the child's mother, had denied him access since birth. She refused to tell Dale about the delivery so that she could omit his name from the birth certificate.

Dale sensed a new beginning now that he had a legal right to see his son and grounds to change the birth certificate. He wanted the world to know that he is a father and that Cody is his son.

Dale imagined all of the wonderful things that he would share with his son. The proud father rushed over to Adalina to indicate that there were no hurt feelings and hugged his 11 month old son. He held up the child and boldy declared, "This is my son!"

The Father of heaven and earth declared that Jesus Christ is His son. At the moment of baptism, the Father could have yelled commands for us to follow Jesus. He could have provided doctrines for holiness and righteousness. The Lord could have even revealed other truths about baptism and keeping covenants; yet, He simply stated that He loved His son and was well pleased.

Through baptism we publicly die to self and publicly declare that we are born again and that we are His. Not only does the Lord fill us with His spirit, but He also declares His love for us and pleasure in us. God will chase us and go through trial after trial to prove that He is our father and that He loves us. His paternity should never be in doubt!

<u>CROSS EXAMINATION</u> – *Examined by the Cross*

1. *Have you received the love from your Father?*
2. *Do you know that He will chase you time and time again even when His paternity has been tested? He has legal rights to you and loves to acknowledge you as His own.*
3. *Have you been baptized into His love?*
4. *Have you felt Him saying that He loves you and is well pleased with you?*

"Now at last we can say the Lord's Prayer without hypocrisy. Previously the words had a rather hollow sound; now they ring with new and wonderful meaning. God is indeed our Father in heaven, who knows our needs before we ask and will not fail to give good things to his children."
John Stott

Day 67

Our Daily Bread

**Jesus answered, "It is written:
'Man does not live on bread alone,
but on every word
that comes from the mouth of God.'"
Matthew 4:4 - NIV**

Stuart had been unemployed for over ten months after having been downsized from a midsize insurance defense firm in Houston, Texas. He could not help but to scream, "Hallelujah!" when he received a call from the temp agency. The temp job enabled him to earn a steady $30 dollars an hour for a guaranteed 60 hours a week and double time after the first 40 hours. He would finally be able to pay his monthly bills as well as his student loans.

As Stuart walked into the firm, he greeted the office manager with a nervous smile. He worried about whether his research skills needed polishing and if they were up to par for the two month document review project. The office manager led Stuart into a room with nine other temps.

"We need you to go through each of these binders and verify that the Bates number on each page goes from 00001 – 10000. There can't be any pages missing," instructed the office manager with a wink.

Stuart looked around the room and saw temps: playing games on their mobile phones, discussing celebrity gossip, and some actually flipping through the pages in the binders. He was in total shock. He could not understand why he was being paid good money for nonsense work.

"I'm confused. The temp agency said that this job required an attorney that was licensed with the Texas Bar. I don't understand. . . this work is kind of. . . "

"Basic? I hope it isn't beneath you. I can contact the temp agency if you aren't comfortable here," threatened the office manager.

"No, I'm not saying that. I was just curious, but I'll give it a shot and see how . . . " said Stuart trying to walk back his comments. The office manager introduced him to the other temps, then left the room.

"That was smooth. You almost blew a really good thing for yourself!" laughed Hiro a middle aged temp. Hiro was the oldest of the group. Everyone seemed comfortable in business casual dress while Stuart wore a suit and tie. Stuart realized that he had offended his supervisor, but held his position that there was something shady about making $2,400 a week for such basic work.

"You obviously haven't temped much. A lot of these jobs are scams. The firms require temps to have a law degree and to be licensed in Texas, so they can bill clients at $300 per hour for unnecessary legal work. The temp agency provides the firms an independent accounting of the manufactured hours while the temps do no real legal work. They pay the temp agency $100 an hour and we get $30 an hour," Hiro explained as a debate ensued. Some of the temps wanted to change the subject to protect a "good thing," while others wanted to chime in on their experiences on different temp assignments and being part of the "scam."

Stuart lamented the conversation that he would have with his girlfriend that evening. The temp job fueled hopes of getting back on his feet and buying an engagement ring, but this appeared to be a high level scam. His girlfriend, Naahla, had put up with his unemployment for a while. He struggled with the thought of turning down close to ten thousand dollars a month for two months. He had been unemployed for almost a year and now had easy money: money that he deserved and money that seemed like manna from heaven. He could even job search through his smart phone while "working" as a temp.

Stuart, then, debated the ethics of quitting. If he quit, then he would not be able to pay debts. He could either keep his unethical job and pay bill collectors or quit his job and be unethical and unable to pay creditors. He kept hearing the words, "Love your neighbor as yourself" in his mind. Even if the firm's client was a big corporation in an anti-trust case who probably deserved to be cheated, Stuart knew in his spirit that it would be wrong to help the firm scam clients.

"Well, I guess you won't be living just off of principal, but living off the word of God and His promises," encouraged Naahla as she remembered the scriptural account of Satan's temptation of Jesus in the wilderness. His girlfriend apologized for anything she may have said that tempted him to even consider crossing his faith. The next morning, Stuart resigned from the temp agency.

Satan lies to us daily that real life makes biblical principles impractical so we must compromise our faith. Jesus Christ is our daily bread and is sufficient to supply all of our needs according to His riches in glory.

As Jesus responded to Satan in Matthew 4:4, he referred to the "*rhema*" word of God. Man does not live off of bread alone but the *rhema* word of God. *Rhema* refers to an utterance or spoken word of the Holy Spirit that meets people where they are and with what they need.

Stuart remembered the *logos* word ("Love your neighbors as yourself") and ate from the *rhema* word ("The firm clients are your neighbors, do not be part of this scam"). A preacher may preach from the *logos* (written word of God) and the listener may be led by the Holy Spirit to think and feel other things. The listener is experiencing the *rhema* word as he/she encounters the Holy Spirit. **Our daily bread is more than food, it is the body that was broken and it is the word that is spoken from the mouth of God.**

CROSS EXAMINATION - *Examined by the Cross*

1. *Have you ever had a situation in which you had to walk in faith and rely on God's logos word (the Bible)?*
2. *Have you ever had a situation in which you had to walk in faith and rely on God's rhema word (the Holy Spirit)?*

"If there is a need, He supplies it.
If there is a wound, He cures it.
If there is a doubt, He destroys it."
Hazem Farraj

Day 68

No Congeniality Awards

**"This is to my Father's glory,
that you bear much fruit,
showing yourselves to be my disciples."
John 15:8 - NIV**

In seconds, Joaquin realized that the performance review was not going to go well. He had been a great team player in terms of boosting firm morale. Joaquin participated on the firm softball team, hung out at happy hours and other get-togethers, and even started a social media page for the firm.

The partners gave him faint praise for the "extras" that he brought the company; yet, reprimanded him for his poor billable hours. Joaquin did not bring in enough money to cover his salary.

"There is no Ms. Congeniality award in law firms. I want to work with likeable people, but we need people who bring in money to sustain our operations. You need to be more focused. You have one more month to show a dramatic increase in production. If you don't know how to bring in clients, ask for help," advised Archie Ladersol.

Joaquin continued over the next month being the same jovial person that everyone came to know and to love. He brought in cakes for birthdays and even came up with great ideas to improve the firm webpage. He was soon terminated because of his lack of productivity.

Joaquin was very foolish. Even though he was a good person and worked hard, he was not productive in the manner in which his employer required him to bear fruit. Jesus Christ requires his followers to be fruitful. Christians can take solace in the fact that salvation is based on believing in Jesus; however, believers prove their faith by sharing it. In the parable of the talents, Jesus illustrates the foolishness of a person who bears no return from the things that the Master has provided.[15] It is the foolish Christian who stores up the word of God, yet never invests in it to bear fruit.

In the parable of the sheep and the goats, Jesus provides a prelude to Judgment Day in which people are judged by their actions and inaction.[16] Just like Joaquin's employers, Jesus warns humanity of His definition of fruitfulness and productivity. One does not get into heaven just for being a nice person; moreover, there must be fruit.

---

[15] **Matthew 25:14-30**

[16] **Matthew 25:31-46**

In Mark 11:12-14, Jesus cursed a fig tree for not being fruitful to send a message to the church of inevitable punishment for an unfruitful life. There are parts of the Bible that are troubling or should at least trouble you. Do not follow the path of Joaquin who had a false sense of productivity. The church must produce fruit on the Lord's terms. The church does not dictate terms to the Lord. Jesus calls us to produce fruit that will endure, nothing else matters.

There is no Ms. Congeniality award.

CROSS EXAMINATION – *Examined by the Cross*

1. *Are you a believer? Are you a disciple?*
2. *Are you bearing fruit? Are you bearing much fruit?*
3. *Do you realize that heaven and hell isn't just a separation of the nice from the mean, but a separation of disciples from the apathetic and uninvolved?*

"A church is nothing better than an ethical club if its sympathies for lost souls do not overflow, and it does not go out to seek to point lost souls to the knowledge of Jesus Christ."
George W. Truett

By Gregory D. Yancey, Esq.

Day 69

Watch Your Mouth

**"But I tell you that men will have to give account
on the day of judgment for every careless
word they have spoken.
For by your words, you will be acquitted,
and by your words you will be condemned."
Matthew 12:36-37 - NIV**

Judge Ackerman stared at the defendant and his attorney for a brief second before stating "I find the defendant, John Ray Ballard guilty of breaking and entering the Praether's home. Sir, I am sentencing you to incarceration for two years and requiring restitution in the amount of three thousand dollars to replace the coin collection that you stole."

Bart Mathis, the defense attorney, and John Ray Ballard stood with their mouths fully agape. The Praethers admitted under cross examination that they were not home when their property had been burglarized. The police did not find any stolen property in John Ray Ballard's home. The only real evidence presented was Jenny Praether's testimony that she lost her key the day before the break-in at the Ballard's home while playing with Tanya Ballard.

"You're probably wondering how I determined your guilt? Mr. Ballard, you testified that there was no way that you could have broken into the Praether's home. You testified that you wouldn't risk taking 19 mm slugs from a Glock-17 in your body for some Civil War era coins. The police report simply refers to antique coins and the officer never testified to the coins as being from the Civil War era. I also find it interesting that you knew the exact kind of gun that Mr. Praether keeps in his home," lectured Judge Ackerman. Realizing that his own words had convicted him, Ballard shamefully nodded and acknowledged that he had used the key of his daughter's best friend to steal the antique coins.

On Judgment Day, God will review every word that has ever been spoken. He will evaluate words of *love* and words of *hate*; words of *purity* and words of *profanity*; words of *truth* and words of *lies*; words of the *gospel* and words of *blasphemy*; words of *praise* and words of *complaint*; words of *faith* and words of *doubt*; words of *encouragement* and words of *slander*; words that *showed you knew right from wrong*; and words of *life* and words of *death*. How will your words measure up in judgment? Watch your mouth, guard your tongue, and choose your words carefully.

<u>CROSS EXAMINATION</u> – *Examined by the Cross*

1. *Do you speak as if God is in the room?*
2. *Do you keep promises?*
3. *Do you lie? Do you gossip?*
4. *Do you encourage others?*
5. *Do your words evidence your faith in God?*
6. *Do your words exhibit purity and holiness?*
7. *Would your words condemn you or acquit you on Judgment Day?*
8. *Read the quote below. Do your words reveal your daily spiritual walk in Heaven or in Hell?*

"And that is why, at the end of all things,
when the sun rises here and the twilight turns to blackness down
there, the Blessed will say
'We have never lived anywhere except in Heaven,' and
the Lost, 'We were always in Hell.'
And both will speak truly."
C. S. Lewis

Day 70

THE EMANCIPATION PROCLAMATION

**In the same way, after supper he took the cup, saying,
"This cup is the new covenant in my blood; do this,
whenever you drink it, in remembrance of me."
For whenever you eat this bread and drink this cup,
you proclaim the Lord's death until he comes.
1 Corinthians 11:25-26 - NIV**

"Mommy, you're always working on the proclamation," texted Fiona, irritated about another volleyball game that her mother would miss.

"Fi, this is a different proclamation. I'm the governor's lawyer. I have to write proclamations and review them for the governor from time to time," Cora stated in a responsive text. Cora prided herself for attending three out of the last five games, but she would fall to a fifty percent attendance rate after missing this game. In a series of text messages, Cora explained that a proclamation is an official statement from a government leader. Some proclamations may be symbolic gestures such as declaring a day to honor a local celebrity, while others may have serious implications such as a state of emergency or a treaty.

"Sort of like the Emancipation Proclamation which announced the end of slavery," Fiona offered.

"Exactly, Abraham Lincoln made an official statement to the country. I review proclamations to make sure that the statements are clear, that they don't offend anyone, and that we have the authority to make the statement," Cora added.

Cora looked up at the portrait on her office wall depicting The Lord's Supper. She, then, realized that Jesus had made a proclamation and encouraged all believers to declare it as well. Communion provides a time to reflect upon the sacrifice that Jesus made through His shed blood and His broken body. Communion is also a *proclamation* that our risen Savior shall return. Jesus said "For whenever you eat this bread and drink this cup, you proclaim the Lord's death until he comes."

Christians not only proclaim their faith in His return, but their intent to be prepared for the soon coming King.

Communion is an emancipation proclamation even greater than the official statement made by Abraham Lincoln. The King of Kings declared freedom from sin and the grave over the heirs to the throne.

CROSS EXAMINATION – *Examined by the Cross*

We have been freed by the breaking of the body and the shedding of the blood.

In communion with the Lord:

Proclaim your emancipation from evil thoughts;
Proclaim your emancipation from evil deeds;
Proclaim your emancipation from evil speech; and
Proclaim your emancipation from evil people!
Who the Son sets free is free indeed!

Proclaim emancipation from one thing that binds you.
(fear, addiction, overeating, lust, low self-esteem, etc.)

"Communion is that state where man seeks to live in the will of God, the wonder of God. Communion necessitates that two must covenant themselves, two must agree. Communion is that power which comes to a person whose life really pleases the Lord. Wherever there is communion there is power."
Rev. Dr. Harold A. Carter

Day 71

CIRCUS COURT

"But with loud shouts they insistently demanded
that he be crucified, and their shouts prevailed.
So Pilate decided to grant their demand.
He released the man who had been thrown into prison
for insurrection and murder,
the one they asked for, and
surrendered Jesus to their will."
Luke 23:23-25 - NIV

"That's why we call it 'Circus Court' instead of Circuit Court," screamed Connie Hangul as she exited the court building and entered the courtyard.

"We can appeal this, right? How can a person go to jail for just using a computer?" Yoo Jeon asked as he tried to deal with the thought of his sister, Cho Hee, spending the next twenty years in jail for possession of child pornography. The forensic analysis showed that Cho Hee never downloaded any photos; in fact, the case hinged on one click of the button and an alleged attempt to access pornography. The evidence at trial showed that Cho Hee never visited a porn site, but that either a pop-up link or a virus infected Cho Hee's browser and redirected her away from the website that she had intended to search. In clicking the "x" to close the pop up, she opened the entire file.

Connie believed she should have won the case on her cross-examination alone. She cornered Detective Elvin Seneche, the officer from the Task Force of Missing and Exploited Children, into admitting that the department lured predators through computer viruses that caused links to child porn to randomly pop-up on the browser that Cho Hee used. The officer admitted that he arrested Cho Hee based on tracking software that was contained in the virus. Cho Hee could have accidentally clicked the link to the child porn. The Task Force kicked in her door based on a single click.

"Appeals are expensive and it is very hard to convince the appellate court that the *Circus Court* made a legal error of law and abused its discretion. The case never should have made it to a jury. Unfortunately, I don't see an appellate court overturning a jury decision on a child predator case," Connie explained. Cho Hee stayed in prison for seven years before being released.

After years of complaints, the State eventually acknowledged that investigators had been overzealous in prosecuting child predators and had criminalized innocent people. Defenders of the program claimed that they were responding to the demands of the masses who wanted to protect children at all costs even though they had entrapped innocent civilians through computer viruses.

Several years after release, Cho Hee received a large settlement from the State. The young lady told family and friends that although she lost part of her life, she now better understood the injustice that Jesus suffered. Pilate had no evidence of a crime; yet, he responded to the will of the people.

Detective Seneche had no evidence of wrongdoing; he simply responded to the people's desire to arrest child predators even if innocent people were also arrested.

Even though many believed that the crucifixion of Christ would make a nation safer, the Pharisees and the government of Rome committed a crime in killing Jesus. Justice must be determined on grounds of morality not expediency; otherwise, everyone can expect to have more Circus Courts.

CROSS EXAMINATION – *Examined by the Cross*

1. *Have you ever been punished for something that you did not do?*
2. *Did the situation make you question yourself and whether you should have done the wrong thing since you were punished anyway?*
3. *Did the situation make you question God and His divine justice for allowing it to happen?*

Day 72

EVIL IN GREEN TIMES

**"For if men do these things when the tree is green,
what will happen when it is dry?"
Luke 23:31 - NIV**

"It's a win today, but trust me there'll be no rest for the wicked and certainly none for the righteous," remarked Miguel Erickson as he explained to reporters his outlook on the Food and Drug Administration's big victory against Silvostone GMA Farms. Silvostone genetically modified apples to prevent insects from eating their crops. The public initially deemed the genetically modified food to be a safer alternative to pesticides; however, the fruit caused severe intestinal failures, stomach bleeding, and immune system collapses.

Miguel puzzled over the fact that Silvostone Farms enjoyed record breaking profits in apple sales prior to switching to harmful genetic modification practices. "I'm saddened today. If the successful businesses have fallen into greed and corruption, what hope do we have for the struggling farmers and the producers who experience drought and poor crops?" lamented the winning litigator.

Miguel remembered Jesus' admonition to weeping women who cried for Him. As He was led to the crucifixion, the Savior told them not to weep for him, but to weep for themselves as the days of evil advance. If men could act in such wickedness in the presence of the Holy One, we should expect even more evil to come when the Lord is absent.

Even in green times, people lie, cheat, steal and oppress. The Church must remind people that there is no future in evil and that righteousness will be rewarded. Stay vigilant and alert because in dry times there will be even greater contempt for God, the Word of God, and the people of God.

Jesus prophesies of the days ahead in which the wicked will prosper. Dry times are ahead when there will be fewer Christian programming, Christian songs, or Christian films. The presence of the Spirit and godly people will be scarce as unchecked evil appears to thrive. Do not weep for the Lord or the word of God, for heaven neither loses nor experiences a losing season. The unmitigated and undiluted word of God shall remain the standard regardless of our times; therefore, the Church must work all that much harder to seek the Standard Bearer and to teach truth over moral relativism.

CROSS EXAMINATION - *Examined by the Cross*

1. *A person who commits a crime right after being told the law, does evil in green times. A person who tells an unnecessary lie or who steals when they already have enough also commits evil in green times. Why do people commit evil in green times?*
2. *How could people commit evil in the presence of Jesus Christ?*
3. *Do you know anyone who is committing evil in green times?*
4. *Why does Jesus warn the women in Luke 23 to be concerned about even greater evil in dry times?*
5. *What can you do to stand against evil?*

"God gives you the strength to press
against the pressure that's pressing you!"
Joyce Meyers

Day 73

A CROSS TO BEAR

**"Verily, verily, I say unto you.
Except a corn of wheat fall into the ground
and die, it abideth alone: but if it die,
it bringeth forth much fruit.
He that loveth his life shall lose it;
and he that hateth his life in this world
shall keep it unto life eternal."
John 12:24-25 - KJV**

Sharon Rose stared at her client, Drake Charoenkul, in total disbelief as the two walked past the metal detectors. Sharon felt sorry for the young man falsely accused of robbing a gas station and took his case on a *pro bono* basis. Drake, a seventeen year old, worked two jobs while taking care of his sickly mother and three younger siblings. He had been so responsible in all areas of his life, yet he came to court on the day of trial without the bank records which confirmed his alibi and without his girlfriend, a key witness, who could verify that he had been at a restaurant on the evening of the robbery.

Sharon had spoken with Drake's girlfriend weeks ago and she even spoke to a waiter at the restaurant where the two dined twenty miles away from the gas station. The case had been postponed previously because of the fact that Drake did not have legal counsel, so there was no way that the judge would allow another continuance.

"My girlfriend's boss would not let her take off," Drake explained with equal frustration and disappointment.

Without any evidence of an alibi, Sharon knew that the young man would be convicted. Her heart melted at the thought of Drake's mother and siblings falling down like dominoes if Judge Seiler sentenced Drake to jail.

Sharon answered as the court reporter called the case and immediately asked to be heard before the State could present the case against her client.

"Your Honor, with great shame and embarrassment, I must apologize to the court for the defective counsel that I have provided my client. We had a key witness in this matter and critical evidence which would have confirmed my client's innocence; yet, I failed to issue subpoenas," Sharon plead with a sincerity that silenced the courtroom. She insisted that her client would be denied his right to due process if the trial proceeded.

"Counselor, although I appreciate your candor and willingness to accept responsibility for your actions, I attest that you have not only failed your client but you have also failed the citizens of this state as an officer of the court. The State had witnesses prepared to testify and now because of your incompetence, we will have to postpone this matter. I will continue this case to give Mr. Char-oen-kul. . ., please forgive me if I mispronounced your name, adequate time to hire competent counsel," snapped Judge Seiler.

Judge Seiler held Sharon in contempt of court and scheduled a hearing to determine the appropriate sanctions. Seiler also assured Sharon that he would report her to the Attorney Grievance Commission and recommend action against her license.

Sharon lost a substantial amount of money and credibility in having to retain an attorney to protect her license. Few attorneys would sacrifice a career for a last minute *pro bono* client. Drake felt horribly about the suffering his attorney experienced, but he brought his girlfriend and his bank account records to the re-scheduled hearing. It did not seem right to have his lawyer treated like a criminal just so that he could avoid a jail sentence.

Sharon Rose bore a cross for her client. She accepted unjust punishment to spare her client tremendous pain. The Lord warns us that whoever tries to save his life will lose it, and whoever loses his life will save it. We are called to be living sacrifices for our brothers and sisters. Unlike Sharon Rose, Jesus Christ, the Rose of Sharon, was faultless and died for our salvation.

CROSS EXAMINATION – *Examined by the Cross*

1. *How do you die to self daily?*
2. *What cross have you carried?*
3. *Have you ever sacrificed yourself for another?*
4. *Read the quote below. What is the cost of grace? What makes grace valuable?*

"Cheap grace is preaching forgiveness without requiring repentance, baptism without church discipline, communion without confession. . .
Cheap grace is grace without discipleship, grace without the cross, grace without Jesus Christ, living and incarnate."
Dietrich Bonhoeffer

Day 74

Committed Spirit

**"Jesus called out with a loud voice,
'Father, into your hands I commit my spirit.'
When he had said this, he breathed his last."
Luke 23:46 - NIV**

Black metal crashed once again against the side of J.P.'s head. His assailant, apparently tired from hitting him, turned the barrel of the gun towards the young lawyer's forehead.

Although lightheaded from the blows, J.P.'s thoughts turned away from the wife and children that he loved so dearly, to his purpose. He knew the risks in coming to this neighborhood and asking questions about the Sean Infurnari killing. The residents of the apartment complex either refused to open their doors or claimed not to have seen anything. This one individual in a blue baseball hat responded violently to a few questions. J.P. figured that just like Sean Infurnari, he would be killed without anyone seeing anything.

"You can't take my life. I gave it to God," J.P. said as he felt his head caving inwards. Despite the throbbing within his skull and increasingly blurry vision, J.P. started thinking about a scene from his church's Easter play in which Jesus said:

"The reason my Father loves me is that I lay down my life –
only to take it up again.
No one takes it from me, but
I lay it down of my own accord.
I have authority to lay it down and
authority to take it up again.
This command I received from my Father."
John 10:17-18 - NIV

J.P.'s words puzzled his assailant, defused his assailant's anger, and swung a powerful sword against demonic principalities in the atmosphere.

"You're not a cop? Who are you?" the assailant asked as he lowered the barrel of the gun away from the attorney's head. J.P. introduced himself as "John Paul" before explaining that he had been hired by Sean's widow to investigate the circumstances of his death and to file a civil suit. Sean had no criminal background; yet, the officer claimed that he observed Sean dealing drugs before the confrontation and shooting.

"That guy talked just like you, about God – and not being afraid of anything. He grew up in the projects, but came back to talk to people about God. My sister's friend, Tracy, says the cops shot him cuz he carried one of those small Bibles and must've thought it was a gun. The cop was roughin' up this guy they call 'Swag' and Sean was like 'Is all that necessary?' and they shot him," said the assailant as he placed his gun into his coat pocket.

The King Heights resident introduced himself as Marlon and led J.P. down the hallway to Tracy's apartment. Tracy smiled nervously towards J.P. ignoring the fact that she had previously told him that she had not seen anything. The tiny woman in nurse's scrubs offered the young attorney a cool towel for his bloodied and bruised head.

J.P.'s committed spirit and willingness to die gave Tracy the courage to come forward and testify against Officer Staples. Tracy told people that she put her life into God's hands. At first, Tracy's bravery seemed to be in vain after Officer Staples' acquittal; however, several months later the press reported that the officer took his life after being unable to live with himself. Sean's widow took no joy in the officer's suicide, but felt vindicated by the civil suit settlement and acknowledgement by other officers from the police department of the crime that had been committed against her husband.

Imagine what would have happened if J.P. feared pursuing justice. In the moments in which he took blows on the head, it must have appeared that evil prevailed. Evil appeared to prevail when Officer Staples was acquitted; however, J.P. and Tracy overcame the fear of death to expose injustice.

Jesus defeated death and the grave even though evil appeared to have won. Do not get discouraged when evil appears to win. Do not fear anyone or any system that can kill the body. No one can take your life when you freely give it to the Lord Almighty. The enemy had no power over Jesus since he sacrificed His life. The enemy has no power over you when you do likewise.

CROSS EXAMINATION - *Examined by the Cross*

1. *Have you ever confronted danger and been willing to place your life into God's hands?*
2. *What are you willing to die for?*
3. *What did J.P. have that was more powerful than Marlon's gun?*

"Eighty-six years have I served Him, and He has done me no wrong: how then can I blaspheme my Savior and King?"
Polycarp *prior to being executed for his faith*

Day 75

The Lord Keeps Moving

**"The angel said to the women,
'Do not be afraid,
for I know that you are looking for Jesus,
who was crucified."
Matthew 28:5 - NIV**

H ialeah cleared her throat as she addressed the board. She wondered why everything felt so off today. The board members usually laughed at her jokes and normally welcomed her with open arms. In previous exchanges, the board treated their in-house counsel like a rock star, yet everyone seemed intense and concerned.

An employee had threatened to sue the company on grounds of age discrimination and sexual harassment after a manager reduced her responsibilities and made inappropriate jokes about hot flashes. Hialeah explained that she worked with HR and terminated the manager. Although unable to convince the employee to stay with the company, Hialeah offered a substantial severance package which prohibited future law suits against the company.

After an hour of intense questioning, Hialeah calmed numerous concerns and was once again received with open arms. Hialeah realized that even though she entered the same boardroom and encountered the same people, she should not have been surprised by a different experience. The attorney had to work harder and wait longer to enjoy the fellowship of her colleagues.

Just like Hialeah, Christians often expect to find the same experience with God when they walk into the same church, hear the same pastor, or even listen to the same music. It can be highly disappointing to go back to the same church, listen to the same pastor, or listen to the same music and have no encounter with God. Even when we read the same scripture in the Bible, we experience different feelings on different days. Similar to Hialeah's experience, Christians may have to work harder and wait longer to enjoy God's fellowship because *the Lord keeps moving*.

Christians often feel like the women who searched for Jesus at the grave. The women did not expect a dead man to move. Jesus rose. The Lord moved to a new location, encountered the women in a different way, and presumably blessed them even more when they found Him.

By Gregory D. Yancey, Esq.

As the angel advised the women at the tomb, so the angel advises all people of faith, "Do not be afraid for I know that you are looking for Jesus." Your encounter with the Lord was real. He is real. He is alive. You may not have experienced Him lately. You may not have seen Him or felt Him, but you must keep looking, you must keep calling Him, and you must continue to believe. You cannot find Him in dead places or in a past anointing. He will always do new things and take you to greater revelations.

Think of Moses' interactions with the Lord. Moses encountered the Lord at a burning bush, on top of Mt. Sinai, in the Tent of Meeting, and also while set in a cleft of the rock on Mt. Nebo. The Lord keeps moving.

You will find Him and you will be richly rewarded for your faithful diligence. The Lord keeps moving and we are required to move with Him. There are times in which we are to stand still. We may seek Him in a solemn place or a prayer closet, but there is still a spiritual search within us that must occur as we move from the things of this world to the things of the spirit.

The Lord keeps moving.

CROSS EXAMINATION – *Examined by the Cross*

1. *Identify some of the places in which you have encountered the Lord throughout your life?*
2. *In the last 24 hours, how have you searched for the Lord? Where has He moved?*
3. *What can you do to intensify the way in which you seek the Lord? Studying? Praying? Fasting? Serving? Resting? Receiving mentoring? Fellowshipping? Finding solitude?*

Day 76

Go Ye Therefore

"Therefore go and make disciples of all nations,
baptizing them in the name of
the Father
and of the Son
and of the Holy Spirit,
and teaching them to obey everything
I have commanded you.
And surely I am with you always,
to the very end of the age."
Matthew 28:19-20 NIV

After quitting the temp agency, Stuart spent another two months unemployed. The newly licensed attorney's heart raced when he received the offer for a full time position with a Legal Aid organization that enabled him to provide services to those of lesser means. He enjoyed the position even though he often worked 15 hour days and made less money than his friends from law school. Stuart shared his excitement with everyone in his bible study. The brothers and sisters in his group had been praying with Stuart for months that he would find a higher paying job. His girlfriend, Naahla, even fasted at times.

For the last few weeks, Stuart's bible study group explored the Great Commission and made a vow to share the gospel once a month for three months. Stuart felt terribly because every time the group went out to witness he had a work-related conflict that prevented him.

Stuart rationalized that he served God as an attorney and that he could be a good Christian without being in someone's face and handing out tracks. One day while walking from the metro station to his office, Stuart felt an irresistible urge to repent and to apologize to God for not actively sharing his faith and honoring the Great Commission.

"Lord, I'm sorry. You gave me this job and I allowed it to be an excuse for not serving you in all areas in which I can serve you. I promise I'll share the gospel at the first available moment and if one doesn't come soon, then I'll make time," Stuart prayed.

No sooner than Stuart prayed those words, he received a text message that his office had been closed for the day due to a power failure. It was unusual for a power failure in the middle of summer on such a gorgeous day, but he figured that God gave him an opportunity to witness.

Stuart walked downtown trying to muster the courage to share his faith. He rested at a bus stop to strategize and to pray for guidance. As he started to take a seat, he saw a rough looking man in a hoodie who appeared extremely angry.

With a lump in his throat and a pounding heart, Stuart stated the only witnessing words he could think of, "My brother, God has a plan for your life."

The hooded man at the bus stop muttered bitterly, "Wow, now you do this God? Are you serious? Why won't you let me do this? Just let me go." As the man spoke, the volume of his voice reached unrestrained rage.

The man identified himself as Doug and quickly explained his outrage with God and himself. Due to his drug addiction, his wife kicked him out of their home. Doug resided with his mother while going in and out of rehab for over a decade. For several months, his mother saved money from her fixed income with the hopes of traveling to South Carolina to see her dying sister. Doug's mother saved enough money for airfare and for a stay of two months without income. She had planned on purchasing her tickets that week; however, Doug stole his mother's money that morning to buy drugs. Now it appeared that there was no way his mother would be able to see his aunt.

"I was just trying to figure out how to kill myself. I told God that I'm tired of hurting. I'm tired of hurting people. Everything is pointless and then you stepped up to me saying He has a plan for my life," said Doug.

Stuart could not think of any scripture to share. He became disheartened and thought about how people from his bible study group would have been better prepared to help Doug. Stuart prayed silently to himself for the correct words to say to the suicidal man. "Do you have any children? I'm sure they depend on you. They'd miss you if you were gone," Stuart added.

Doug cried about the times that his daughter had to pick him up off the ground in front of her friends when he got drunk or high. "I embarrass her. She'd be better off without me," Doug sniffled.

Stuart realized that there were no correct words needed, he just needed to follow the guidance of the Holy Spirit and to trust the promise that the Lord would be with him to the very end. He had the power of life and death in his tongue. This weakened stranger was now his brother. God commissioned Stuart to tell Doug the good news that heaven had a plan for everyone including a drug addict. Doug remembered that Jesus offered rest to "all ye heavy laden" without discriminating based on criminal misconduct.

"Your mother, daughter, and certainly God – all know about your addiction and still love you. Prove them right to have faith in you. There is a way you can make it up to them, but it'll take time. I wasn't supposed to be here today, but God shut down an office and led me to you, so you're important," Stuart concluded as God changed two lives that day.

Doug focused on the fact that his mother brought an addict into her home and still continued to care for him. His daughter always picked him up when he fell. She even made cookies for him and asked him to promise to eat the cookies instead of taking drugs. Doug sniffled that he could only expect more failures in his life and bringing more hurt to his family.

"How would you feel if I walked up to your mother or your daughter and started hitting them?" Stuart asked.

"I'd beat you down," Doug answered.

"Well, if you kill yourself – you would hurt them more than I ever could. They love you and they believe in you," Stuart concluded his case with a triumphal argument.

The young attorney realized the importance of the Great Commission and bringing the good news to the distressed. Stuart also rejoiced in the promise "surely I am with you always to the very end of this age."

CROSS EXAMINATION – *Examined by the Cross*

1. *Please take the time to pray for more opportunities to do God's work and to have a greater trust that He will work through you to accomplish it in excellence.*

2. *Despite the multitude of churches and tv evangelists, "the harvest is plentiful" and the "laborers are few." See Matthew 9:37. Do you believe this? How would your evangelism change if you truly believed that there was a ripe harvest of people waiting to hear the gospel from you? How would your evangelism change if you truly believed that there are few workers sharing the gospel and not enough to reach the lost?*

"God never calls a person
without giving that person a specific assignment,
a place to carry out the assignment,
and the amazing grace in which to complete the mission."
Rev. Dr. Harold A. Carter

By Gregory D. Yancey, Esq.

t ribulation

r eveals

i ntegrity

a nd

L ord's

S trengthening

CHAPTER 7

TRIALS OF THE SPIRIT

"Now the LORD is the Spirit,
and where the Spirit of the LORD is,
there is freedom."
2 Corinthians 3:17 - NIV

Day 77

ᵭRIVING SPIRIT

**"But if I drive out demons by the Spirit of God,
then the kingdom of God has come upon you."**

Matthew 12:28 - NIV

Tilmon nervously bumped into the chaplain as he followed the prison ministry team down the detention center corridors to the chapel. The compassionate attorney figured this would be a great way to understand the incarcerated population and the available prison-to-workforce resources for his clients who have been released.

To his disappointment, the "chapel" was just a regular room. No stained glass, not even a cross. To his dismay, the chapel also appeared to be unsafe. He could not understand why the guards left chapel and allowed the inmates to interact directly with the volunteers without any supervision. Tilmon tried to remain calm as he walked amongst convicted criminals who had no cuffs or restraints.

"Chaplain Terry, do you feel safe? What if something happens?" the lawyer inquired.

"That's why we're here. We pray for something to

happen. We want the Holy Spirit to move people to be born again," remarked Chaplain Terry.

In 25 years of service, the chaplain never had a violent incident in chapel. Every now and then an inmate would consider causing a disruption, but the presence of the Lord, the singing of hymns, and the peaceful brotherhood usually vexed anyone suffering demonic influence. Troubled inmates typically called the guards and demanded to return to their cells instead of causing a disruption.

"There was one time in 96' when one devil worshipper walked into the middle as we started to form a prayer circle and started yelling out curses and obscenities about Jesus Christ. We closed the prayer circle in on him and prayed for his deliverance. As we got to praying, he ran out of that circle so fast. He ran into the door and pounded on it until the guards let him out," Chaplain Terry recalled as he convinced Tilmon of his safety. The security of the prison ministry never came from the guards or even the weapons carried by the guards. Their safety and security came from the Spirit of the Lord: *the Spirit who drives out demons.*

After his first prayer service in the detention center, Tilmon entered prisons throughout the state with the confidence that he could drive out demons. Even when he met with detained clients, he carried his Bible and rebuked evil spirits. Inmates felt better when they met with him not because of his legal advice, but because of the freedom he gave them from the enemy.

Soon, inmates learned that they could make a claim to the same *driving spirit* that led Tilmon. They could cast out their own demons, demons in other inmates, and even demons that controlled some of the prison guards.

CROSS EXAMINATION – *Examined by the Cross*

1. *Are there any demons that you need to drive out of your life?*
2. *Are there any demons that you need to drive out of others?*
3. *Have you asked God to drive them out?*
4. *Have you sought other Christians for help to drive out demons?*
5. *Which places cause you to fear for your safety? Why?*
6. *Some Christians fear demons while others welcome encounters. Which is the appropriate response? Is there an appropriate middle ground?*

Day 78

The Spirit of Truth

**"When the Counselor comes,
whom I will send to you from the Father,
the Spirit of truth who goes out from the Father,
he will testify about me.
And you also must testify,
for you have been with me from the beginning."**
John 15:26-27 - NIV

" I have no further questions," said the defense attorney as he helplessly shook his head. Counsel realized the futility of trying to shake an unshakeable witness. With amazing recall, the witness testified in great detail about the defendant's shooting of an unarmed man in a parking lot. The testimony not only nailed the defendant to the scene of the crime, but also demonstrated the fact that the defendant knew the victim well enough to have been a passenger in his vehicle. The witness could not answer every question or explain how or why the suspect would shoot his acquaintance; however, he testified with the Spirit of truth by which neither the judge nor the jury questioned his veracity.

The Spirit of truth counsels our soul on the difference between right and wrong. The Spirit of truth provides definitive answers that melt confusion and illuminate darkness. The Spirit of truth only comes from God and testifies to the physical incarnation of God's word through Jesus Christ. The Spirit of truth makes the invisible visible and the incomprehensible comprehensible.

In the same manner in which a great witness determines the outcome of a case and sets the platform for a judge to espouse wisdom and justice, the Holy Spirit testifies to the veracity of the word of God and sets the platform for the Father to rule on the lies of the enemy and all evil doers. The Spirit of truth proclaims that Jesus is the Son of God, died for our sins, and rose from the grave. The Spirit of truth confirms that we are children of God and joint heirs to the kingdom. Any voice in opposition of the Spirit of truth bears the spirit of the antichrist and disseminates lies and confusion.

CROSS EXAMINATION – *Examined by the Cross*

1. *Do you listen to the Spirit of truth?*
2. *Where? When? How?*

Day 79

SPIRITUAL CONVICTION

"When he comes, he will convict the world
of guilt in regard to sin and righteousness and judgment:
in regard to sin, because men do not believe in me;
in regard to righteousness, because I am going to the Father,
where you can see me no longer;
and in regard to judgment, because the prince of this world
now stands condemned."
John 16:8-11 - NIV

Titus vehemently argued for the judge to reconsider the decision to give his client, a mere get-away driver, the same sentence as the arsonist who actually destroyed property and murdered innocent people. The judge explained the fact that justice requires an accomplice to a crime to receive the same punishment as the principal actor.

Men and women who refuse to accept Jesus as the Son of God share in Satan's crime. They ignore the word of God, the Spirit of truth, and the love of God. The apathetic and the wicked will receive sentencing for failing to repent and failing to lead others to repentance. **If a man fails to yell "fire" when a building burns, then he is an accomplice to the inferno. As we fail to warn others of the lake of fire, we become accomplices to hell fire. God will judge us.**

Jesus invites everyone to be joint laborers in spreading the gospel and leading others to salvation. Those lacking spiritual fervor will be considered a co-conspirator in Satan's efforts to populate the lake of fire. Scripture leaves no room for apathy and no room for neutrality. Every individual is either a child of light or a child of darkness.

The Spirit of truth will convict the world of its guilt. The gospel clearly reveals that God so loved the world that He gave His only begotten son and that our salvation depends on our belief in Him.[17] The Spirit slices a dividing line between believers and nonbelievers and the righteous and the wicked.

John 16:8-11 states that the prince of this world stands condemned and that others will be condemned because they did not believe Jesus. If the apathetic had believed Jesus, then they would have loved the Lord with all of their hearts, minds, and strength. The apathetic and indifferent would love their neighbors as themselves.

---

[17] John 3:16

Inaction only maintains the status quo and secularism. Hold onto your *spiritual conviction* (beliefs, doctrine, faith) to avoid the *final conviction* (sentencing, punishment, judgment) that awaits the world. Sound the alarm for truth! Sound the alarm for repentance! Sound the alarm for the kingdom of God! Be an accomplice for heaven!

CROSS EXAMINATION – *Examined by the Cross*

1. *Are you an accomplice to heaven or to hell?*
2. *Do your words and action inspire belief or disbelief in God?*
3. *What is the spirit of conviction? Does it seem extreme?*
4. *Why is there a punishment for not believing Jesus Christ? Please read John 16:8-11.*
5. *What other sins or actions can be tied to not believing Jesus Christ?*

"Reducing the human job description
down to one phrase, and this is it:
reflect God's glory."
Max Lucado

Day 80

Just Ask

> "Which of you fathers, if your son asks for a fish,
> will give him a snake instead?
> Or if he asks for an egg, will give him a scorpion?
> If you then, though you are evil,
> know how to give good gifts to your children,
> how much more will your Father in heaven
> give the Holy Spirit to those who ask him!"
> **Luke 11:11 - NIV**

"Just ask," Juliet Bledsoe insisted.

"The case is over. We won – let's just go," Desmond whispered back as he shuffled his papers before placing them into his trial bag. He had successfully won a contempt action in his client's behalf after her ex-husband refused to pay child support payments for several months. Judge Silas Winnipeg hit Mr. Bledsoe with a whopping judgment for child support arrears plus attorneys fees. Mr. Bledsoe had thirty days to make a $6,000 payment towards back child support or face incarceration.

"Could you please just ask?" Juliet politely demanded.

"Is everything okay?" Judge Winnipeg asked after noticing that Ms. Bledsoe and her attorney appeared to be in a dispute.

"I appreciate your decision and I'm thankful. I was just wondering if my son's Boy Scouts troop could visit your courtroom one day and see what it's like to be a judge. They are required to visit a government institution to get a badge. I thought this would be good for them. . . that is. . . if you have any age appropriate cases that they can hear," inquired Juliet as her attorney blushed. Desmond warned her that this was entirely inappropriate and low class. He figured that she would have to hear it directly from the judge to believe it.

"I'd enjoy that a lot. That's a great idea. People only see judges and courtrooms during negative experiences. I love it! They can shadow me next month when I have the juvenile docket. They can see our chambers and even visit the jail. Milton, my law clerk, will provide you the contact number for my chambers. Tuesdays and Thursdays would be ideal days for a tour and for sitting in my courtroom," laughed Judge Winnipeg as he gave Juliet the Boy Scouts salute. Juliet elbowed her attorney in his ribs and then extended the Boy Scouts salute. Milton handed Juliet a post-it with the phone number to Judge Winnipeg's chambers.

Desmond had argued cases for three decades in the county without ever asking if any of the children in his youth group could tour the courthouse.

Desmond thought about all the opportunities for himself and his youth groups that he had missed over the years simply because he never asked the judge.

Christians miss out on much more when they fail to ask the Father for things in prayer. Jesus tells us that we can ask the Father for the gift of the Holy Spirit. We have the means to obtain spiritual gifts of understanding, wisdom, prophesy, preaching, healing, teaching, evangelism, encouragement, administration, and gifts of tongues if we just ask.

CROSS EXAMINATION - *Examined by the Cross*

1. *Have you asked the Lord for the gifts of the Holy Spirit? Have you asked Him to improve a gift?*
2. *Do you understand that you can have access to the Father and to the kingdom?*
3. *Do you understand that you can use these gifts to win souls and empower others?*
4. *What is holding you back from asking?*
5. *What opportunities do you think Desmond missed? What opportunities have you missed by failing to ask God for a spiritual gift?*

Day 81

ADVERSE POSSESSION

"When an evil spirit comes out of a man,
it goes through arid places seeking rest and does not find it.
Then it says, "I will return to the house I left.'
When it arrives, it finds the house swept clean and put in order.
Then it goes and takes seven other spirits more wicked than itself,
and they go in and live there.
And the final condition of that man is worse than the first."
Luke 11:24-26 NIV

"You can't just let the property sit that's why we have drug addicts, squatters, and all kinds of people in it. They pretty much own it through adverse possession unless you kick them out and get someone in it. I tried to tell you this when you had me evict the church!" Clarabelle Barrowman snapped in a failed attempt to avoid the *"I Told You So"* tone.

Four years ago, her client, Growth Goat Capital ("GGC"), paid 1.5 million dollars to acquire a 2.5 million dollar note that Hamilton Steele Bank held against a struggling church. The church had fallen two months behind on their mortgage, so Hamilton Steele renegotiated the loan and had an oral agreement for lower payments. GGC bought the note and refused to honor the oral agreement because of the prospect of flipping the property and making a quick million dollar profit with a developer.

Unfortunately for GGC, the developer underestimated construction costs and failed to complete the job. GGC lacked the funds to hire another contractor and even lacked the money to prevent squatters from entering the property. Instead of getting consistent mortgage payments from a church, they now received nothing on a property occupied by trespassers. The law of adverse possession means that a trespasser can eventually own property if the owner fails to evict the person timely. GGC now has to constantly monitor the property and pay to have people removed. The police refuse to act as security guards in the bad neighborhood.

Jesus warns everyone of a greater property that can be adversely possessed by trespassers: our bodies. Unless we are filled with the Holy Spirit, demonic spirits and principalities will make their homes inside of us. Unless your mind and heart are filled with God's righteousness and holiness, they will become strongholds for all kinds of evil. It isn't enough to go to church occasionally, read scripture occasionally, or to pray occasionally to evict evil from your mind, heart, and life. You must allow the Holy Spirit to be a permanent resident and leave no vacancy for evil. Just as it is a bad investment for a real estate company to have empty buildings, it is a bad investment to have a life that is empty of the Holy Spirit and the love of God.

GGC wanted to own more than a "church property" and ended up with an abandoned building. Some people want more than being a "goodie goodie Christian" and end up serving evil. Do not be adversely possessed. Be occupied by the Holy Spirit!

CROSS EXAMINATION – *Examined by the Cross*

1. *Have you ever seen an abandoned building that had been adversely possessed and made worse?*
2. *What activities do you engage in to stay filled with the Holy Spirit?*
3. *What do you do to fill your mind, your heart, and your life with the things of God?*
4. *Do you have children, nieces/nephews, or friends that you try to fill with goodness to protect them from adverse possession?*

"You cannot have peace as long as demons control your life.
They will always lead you astray.
They will direct your path away from God.
When you are cleansed, you need the Holy Spirit to fill every corner of your life so that evil spirits have no place to dwell."
Mary Baxter

Day 82

"Yes" and "Amen"

"For no matter how many promises God has made,
they are "Yes" in Christ.
And so through him the "Amen" is spoken
by us to the glory of God."
2 Corinthians 1:20 - NIV

Clint Peydu took a deep breath as he flipped through his Bible hoping he would find the scripture that he needed to read. Clint had a comfortable, yet unexciting job at the firm. He struggled with whether he should accept an offer from a former client to become a lobbyist. The position offered more money and power to make a greater difference, but Clint feared embarking on a new career path at his age. The aroma of his half eaten dinner filled the office as the cleaning crew vacuumed. The older attorney often dove into scripture as a nice break in the midst of trial prep.

"The devil has more faith in God, than you do," said an older woman from the cleaning crew as she emptied the waste basket.

"Excuse, me?" puzzled Clint.

"I'm just saying. We pray. We ask for confirmation. We get confirmation. Then, we question God. Isn't that what Moses did when God told him to lead the people out of slavery?" commented the cleaning woman.

Clint had never spoken to the custodian before and could not understand why she felt no need to address him in a professional manner. *How could she say that Satan had more faith in God than he did?*

"Moses doubted God. He even asked God to send someone else. But what happened when God told Satan that he could take everything from Job, but not to touch Job? The devil did it!" yelled the cleaning woman finding excitement in answering her own question.

"What happened when the Lord told Satan that he could touch Job, but had to spare the man's life? There were no questions. . .no doubting. The devil did it!" litigated the cleaning woman as she built her case.

"Yes, but Satan is a spiritual, supernatural being," rebutted Clint not wanting to seem outsmarted.

"But so are we! Aren't you a spiritual, supernatural being? When Jesus says 'Yes' all we need is for our spirit to say 'Amen' and do it!" laughed the custodian.

Her pastor had preached that Sunday from Job on the topic of ridiculous faith. She enjoyed the message so much that she shared it with everyone she encountered that week.

"There's something wrong if Satan has more faith in God than you do," smiled the cleaning woman. As the woman left the room, she vowed to have ridiculous faith in God and encouraged Clint to possess the same.

Clint pondered her words as he looked at the offer letter. He had prayed for awhile to find greater fulfillment in his work, but never anticipated a career as a lobbyist. One of his former clients started a lobbying group and reached out to Clint based on his solid advocacy skills. God had answered Clint's prayers with a resounding "Yes," so Clint yelled a loud "Amen" to his new calling.

CROSS EXAMINATION - *Examined by the Cross*

2 Corinthians 1:20 describes a binding contract. Once God says, "Yes" all we have to do is say, "Amen."

Not only do we need wisdom from God to know what to request, but we also need the Holy Spirit to recognize when our request has been granted and to act upon it.

1. *Is God waiting for you to say "amen" to something?*
2. *Is God waiting for you to say "amen" to a closer relationship, an assignment, or a calling?*
3. *Are you willing to ask Him and find out?*

Day 83

SPIRITUAL OUTPOURING

"'In the last days,
God says, 'I will pour out my Spirit on all people.
Your sons and daughters will prophesy,
your young men will see visions,
your old men will dream dreams.
Even on my servants, both men and women,
I will pour out my Spirit in those days,
and they will prophesy.'"
Acts 2:17-18 - NIV
(Peter quoting Joel 2;28-32 on the day of Pentecost)

"**I**'m scared for you, what if he wants to fight you?" Cornel asked as he escorted his attorney, Mallory Schultz around the side of his house. Cornel wished the firm had sent a male attorney to deal with Chip Odom of Odom Custom Builders. Chip failed miserably to build the home according to the plans. The abrasive foul-mouthed brute dared Cornel to "do something about it" throughout the construction process.

On one occasion members from the Odom construction crew had to hold Chip back from assaulting Cornel. Cornel feared that the cigar chomping, loud mouth cursing contractor would run roughshod over his petite Christian female attorney. Mallory used words like "blessed" and "prayerful" and lacked an angry bone in her body.

"I've dealt with all types. It's a simple contract issue. He signed a contract agreeing to build in accordance to the plans in Exhibit A. He failed to build a walk-out basement, a balcony, and several other items. We will either receive financial compensation or we will call in the bond and have the house knocked down and built correctly. I will also file a complaint with the Home Improvement Commission and he will lose his license for fraud because he's done this to others. I assure you, he will talk to me," Mallory predicted.

Chip laughed as he approached the two. He smacked the side of the wall as if impressed by his work and then referred to Mallory in a sexually chauvinistic manner. Within minutes, Mallory's predictions manifested. The tough talking contractor offered to add extra accoutrements to the home and to give Cornel a partial refund. Cornel joked that Mallory must be a prophet or something since she knew exactly what would happen. Although confident and led by the Lord, Mallory had no gift of prophecy.

Prophecy is an amazing phenomenon in the church. It goes beyond merely speaking out of hope or making predictions. The Lord actually selects certain people to be His voice and to tell future events. They are His prophets.

Some prophets see visions or experience instructive dreams, while others directly hear the voice of God. Prophets not only reveal the future, they often reveal God's heart. In the days ahead, God will demonstrate more signs and wonders even in the midst of great evil and opposition to provide further opportunities for repentance and salvation.

In addition to studying God's word and fellowshipping with godly people, seek His spirit. God can impart the gift of prophecy, prophetic revelation, or even insight to His personal plan for your life.

Christians must avoid two dangerous extremes. Some people seek prophets like fortune tellers and hope to become god over their own lives, while others disregard prophecy completely as some sort of pagan sideshow. These spiritual outpourings reveal His glory, His goodness, and His grace.

Cʀᴏss Eхᴀᴍɪɴᴀᴛɪᴏɴ – *Examined by the Cross*

1. *Have you ever met a prophet?*
2. *Have you ever had someone prophecy over your life?*
3. *Have you ever read a book on prophecy? Have you ever wondered how to obtain the gift of prophecy?*
4. *How would your life change if you heard a prophetic word? How would you change the lives of others if you gave a prophetic word?*

"A *prophetic word* is a special inspired message or word that a person receives in his or her inner spirit after a season of fasting and extended prayer or, at times, through an inspired utterance from scripture and occasionally confirmed by a vocal gift from another believer."
Perry Stone

Day 84

SPIRITUAL WISDOM

"For who among men knows the thoughts of a man
except the man's spirit within him?
In the same way no one knows the thoughts of God
except the Spirit of God.
We have not received the spirit of the world
but the Spirit who is from God,
that we may understand what God has freely given us.
This is what we speak, not in words taught us by human wisdom but
in words taught by the Spirit,
expressing spiritual truths in spiritual words."
1 Corinthians 2:11-13 - NIV

As her mobile phone rang, Kelly saw a number that

she did not recognize, so she let it go to voice mail. With a

busy schedule, prioritization is essential. Kelly faced too

many number one items that had to get done for her to get

bogged down in a matter that may be trivial. As a sole

practitioner, she could get thirty to forty calls a day from

people soliciting free legal advice about insignificant matters.

The voicemail message revealed a familiar distraught

tone that she had heard many times before from potential

clients who had reached their breaking point. The caller faced

a dead end.

There was no pride in the caller's voice, no inhibitions to protect her dignity, no nonchalant airs, merely cries for help from domestic abuse, emotional abuse, and a financial cliff that stretched before her. Like a child lost in a mall, the caller had no idea of what to do, but knew she needed someone's hand to lead her.

Kelly decided to make the caller her top priority. Before pressing the number to return the call, she closed her eyes, bowed her head, and prayed: *"Heavenly Father, I pray for my sister. I thank You for the trust that You have given me to advise Your daughter and to share Your love and Your heart with her, but Father, there is nothing that I can do apart from You. My schooling and my experience are nothing compared to the favor and power of your Comforter.*

Please help me to reduce in this hour. Strip me of my opinions, perspectives, and biases so I can hear my sister and give her good counsel. Please let me know whether or not this is a client that I should assist or refer to someone else. Please help me to also hear the things that she doesn't say or may be too scared to say. Please help me to discern truth from half-truth and to make every decision based on Your will as opposed to financial gain or fear of financial loss if she has limited means.

I love You, Lord. Please empower me with Your love and Your light in the time I have with my sister. I pray that You will infect her husband with Your light and love as well, so that he will have no desire to hurt her and that she will have no desire to hurt him either. Please bless any children that they may have and their marriage, if sustainable, if not then please help them to go separate ways peacefully. In the name of Jesus Christ, I pray. Amen."

The attorney had over twenty-five years of experience, practicing law. She had been considered to be a great lawyer in the community and she was loved by her clients, yet she always sought counsel from the Holy Spirit before speaking to clients. Sometimes, she would even pray for guidance silently while clients spoke to her.

Jesus promised us the Holy Spirit. The Comforter counsels us, intercedes for us, cleans us, empowers us, and leads us. Lean not on your own understanding, but in every way acknowledge the Lord if you intend to be effective. You need His wisdom. He promises to give generously to everyone who asks.

> **"If any of you lacks wisdom, he should ask God,**
> **who gives generously to all without finding fault,**
> **and it will be given to him."**
> **James 1:5 - NIV**

CROSS EXAMINATION - *Examined by the Cross*

1. *God promises to generously give wisdom to anyone who asks. In which area(s) of your life, do you need wisdom?*
2. *Ask God to give you wisdom in that particular area of your life.*
3. *If you are unable to identify an area, ask God to identify areas in which you need wisdom and to provide you wisdom and discernment.*
4. *Ask God to give wisdom to someone in need of wisdom.*

"We must be willing to leave behind
what we have come to know,
that we may more fully comprehend
what is yet to be known."
Bishop Monroe Saunders, Jr.

Day 85

BLACK AND WHITE

"The acts of the sinful nature are obvious:
sexual immorality, impurity and debauchery; idolatry and witchcraft;
hatred, discord, jealousy, fits of rage, selfish ambition, dissensions,
factions and envy;
drunkenness, orgies, and the like.
I warn you, as I did before, that those who live like this
will not inherit the kingdom of God."
Galatians 5:19-21 - NIV

Trying not to be heard yawning, Eric pressed the mute button on his phone as he tried to gather himself together at 2:07 am. Eric had no reservations whenever it came to his largest client, Vinny Foster, CEO of Straight Thuggin' Entertainment. Vinny indicated that he needed his favorite attorney to negotiate a clothing line for two of his artists.

"I ran into Zeus backstage and he started talkin' about a clothing line for one of my artists and I'm like, *Are you serious?* I'm thinking maybe Buck Wild or Looney. Anyways, we're at a nightclub called The Bank$. They have a private VIP restaurant on the top floor called The Vault$. When you come in the club, ask for the manager and tell him to take you to The Vault$. I need my lawyer! Let's get this inked out, son!" Vinny yelled excitedly.

Eric pressed the mute button again to voice equal excitement about the pending multi-million dollar deal. In less than an hour, Eric dawned his best evening wear and entered the VIP section of The Bank$, an upscale nightspot by the bay. Most people would have complained about a late night or early morning phone call, but Eric wanted to move up in the world.

Vinny slapped Castor Stavros in the back as the two laughed about an altercation between a rap fan and a bouncer at the concert. Castor Stavros, CEO of Zeus Apparel, had also been accompanied by two women who appeared to be models or actresses.

Within moments, Eric listened to Castor's proposed terms of a joint venture agreement. Zeus Apparel wanted to create a clothing line with images of Straight Thuggin' rappers and lettered with song references. As Eric asked questions, he noticed the input offered by the women, Jasmine and Daniella, who accompanied Castor. The women were not models or actresses. They were sophisticated attorneys, yet clung to Castor like groupies. Firm life only netted each of them hundreds of thousands annually, while corporate prostitution netted millions.

Eric felt badly for thinking it, but the ladies seemed like trained Dobermans. They knew when to dumb down for Castor and how to entertain his associates. They laughed when he told a joke. They acted like hostesses at times to make everyone comfortable, but when Castor needed them to be intelligent - they advised him. Eric wondered if they would also attack on command.

"I told you, my man Eric was on point. He'll get the paperwork banged out by noon and we'll get this thing signed before you fly back to London," Vinny boasted while downing another glass of champagne.

"Eric, have you ever been in the presence of such exquisite women? You see I have a black and a white one here in this town. I got Latina honeys, Asian chicks, you name it," Castor laughed. The women knew their cues and laughed as if they weren't offended. Jasmine and Daniella knew everything to say to make Castor happy and flirted with Eric and Vinny equally.

"My friend, you can have either one of them tonight. In fact, why not both?" Castor offered. Vinny informed Eric that more women would join them later and that he would be partaking in the menu that Castor provided. The music mogul gave Eric a quick glance warning his attorney against offending their benefactor.

Vinny had been the once-in-a-lifetime kind of client for Eric. Vinny introduced him to celebrities, business deals, and income unlike any he had ever known. Eric knew it would be wrong to sleep with these women and tried to change the subject often. Eric even joked about the importance of getting a good night sleep to draft the contract; however, Vinny and Castor relentlessly tested his manhood and loyalty. Eric had no respect for the women. Despite their education, he saw them as morally bankrupted prostitutes.

Wealthy shallow people cannot enjoy their success unless they have people to admire them. The two men enjoyed the flattery of the women, but they wanted Eric to envy their financial success and their domination of women. They wanted Eric to sleep with the women that they had already encountered. If Eric refused to sleep with them, then he would reject their lifestyle and their values. Castor and Vinny did not want a conscience nor did they want to be around anyone who had a conscience either. If Eric said "No", he would not only defy them, but he would appear to be looking down on them.

In his mind, Eric rationalized that fornication was probably prohibited in the Bible only because there was no contraception in those days. He thought about the fact that Jasmine and Daniella were consenting adults and he reflected upon all the good work that he had done as a volunteer for legal aid. He ultimately convinced himself that right and wrong was not a matter of black and white.

His business relationship with Vinny and Castor would lead to more money and greater means to do good things. In short, Eric pleased his client instead of pleasing God. The encounter led to a series of downward falls into drugs, financial corruption, and legal malpractice. In the end, he realized that he was as much of a *prostitute* as Jasmine and Daniella. In the end, he became as shallow as Vinny and Castor if not worse for rejecting the one true God for their false gods.

In Galatians 5:17-18, Paul warns us that the sinful nature desires "what is contrary to the Spirit, and the Spirit what is contrary to the sinful nature" and that those who live by the Spirit are not under the law. Eric's desire for wealth and influence caused him to submit to his sinful nature and resist the Spirit of God. Most of the prostitutes in the world do not work the streets in revealing clothing. Moreover, they wear suits and can be found in offices and boardrooms.

By prostituting himself, Eric had also submitted himself to the law of God and judgment. The world tells the Church that there are many shades of grey, but the word of God presents the truth in black and white.

CROSS EXAMINATION – *Examined by the Cross*

1. *Galatians 5:19-21 indicates that the acts of the flesh are obvious, why did things get so complicated for Eric? Why does the difference between right and wrong become less clear in the midst of temptation?*
2. *Why does Paul consider this to be spiritual warfare? Does this mean that there was a war within Eric, a war for Eric, or both?*
3. *Prior to Eric giving in, what threat did he pose to Vinny and Castor? What threat do we pose when we avoid the sinful nature?*
4. *Paul warns us in Galatians 5:19-21 that we will not inherit the kingdom of God if we submit to the acts of the flesh. Besides not getting into heaven, what does this mean?*
5. *Which battles are you fighting against the sinful nature? Which battles have you won? Which battles have you lost? Have you sought help in areas in which you need strength?*

"Holiness does not consist in mystic speculations, enthusiastic fervors, or uncommanded austerities;
it consists in thinking as God thinks and willing as God wills."
John Brown

Day 86

δiplomatic Immunity

**"But the fruit of the Spirit is love, joy,
peace, patience, kindness, goodness, faithfulness,
gentleness and self-control.
Against such things there is no law."
Galatians 5:22-23 NIV**

"How can they just steal from my store? The cops aren't doing anything about it. I don't get it!" Clark yelled through his smart phone as if his attorney could not hear him. A foreign dignitary from the Middle East entered his department store with an entourage of body guards and multiple wives.

The wives tore tag after tag off of various store items and then placed the items in their bags. Some even placed jewelry onto their fingers and wrists. The security guards' efforts to confront the stealing customers were immediately rebuffed by armed body guards of the dignitary.

Clark attempted to involve the police despite the dignitaries repeated yelps of "diplomatic immunity." The police explained to Clark that they could not detain the dignitary or anyone in his entourage; in fact, Clark would be arrested if he even touched the dignitary. Even worse, the body guards could shoot him without impunity.

"Clark, you have to remain calm. The police are correct. Those men can shoot you and no one would even arrest them. Write down everything that they take so we can make an insurance claim," Barbara advised.

"I thought this was America! You got to be kidding me!" Clark erupted as he hung up the phone. Clark fumed and sulked like a child who refused to accept his bedtime. The store owner failed to notice the soft taps on his shoulder from a Middle Eastern man who appeared to be a slightly younger version of the dignitary.

"How do you Americans say it? Put it on my tab? My father says, 'Put it on my tab' for him. Please accept this sir," offered the young dignitary as he handed a stack of traveler checks totaling triple the amount of inventory taken. Clark's eyes bulged like Chihuahua eyes over the checks. He was no longer angry; in fact, he wanted his guests to stay longer.

"Wait! Wait! Can I get a picture?" laughed Clark as he ran to the entourage and insisted that his chief security guard take pictures of him with the dignitary on his smart phone.

Clark later marveled over the fact that state law had no power over his customer. In the same vein, anyone who is filled with the Holy Spirit and bears the fruit of the Spirit enjoys immunity from the law of sin and death. In other words, Christians have diplomatic immunity from the kingdom of darkness.

Believers can take souls from the enemy's stronghold. Believers can also steal hatred, anger, fear, confusion, and even depression from nonbelievers and fill them with love, joy, hope, and peace. Christians have unlimited access to the keys to the kingdom of heaven and victory over sin and the grave. Just like the powerless security guards and police officers in Clark's store, neither Satan nor any of his principalities have any authority over those in Christ Jesus. They may cause temporary hardship, pain, and inconvenience but they have no power over the believer's soul.

The Lord has given believers diplomatic immunity over darkness, over hell, over fear, and over death. The Church must humbly demonstrate the fruits of the Holy Spirit while boldly knowing that against such things "there is no law".

CROSS EXAMINATION – *Examined by the Cross*

1. How much love, joy, peace, forbearance, kindness, goodness, faithfulness, gentleness and self-control do you exhibit daily?
2. Do you have the fruit of the Holy Spirit? Do others see it?
3. What would you steal from the enemy? Will you steal souls? Will you steal someone's hatred and give them love?
4. Will you steal someone's anger and give them joy?
5. Will you steal someone's confusion and give them peace? You have diplomatic immunity, so feel free to steal these things!

"Citizens are born into the earthly city by a nature
spoiled by sin,
but they are born into the heavenly city
by grace freeing nature from sin."
St. Augustine

Day 87

SPIRIT OF FAITH

**"It is written: "I believed; therefore I have spoken."
With that same spirit of faith
we also believe and therefore speak,
because we know that the one who raised the Lord Jesus
from the dead will also raise us with Jesus
and present us with you in his presence."
2 Corinthians 4:13-14 - NIV**

"You know how it is, your Honor. We get along fine it's always our clients," Brittany joked as she sat her bag down on the floor next to her chair. Brittany typically represented the landlord, but in this matter she represented Leigh and Revlynn Chase, two disgruntled tenants who claimed that Lenzaw Ridge Apartments had wrongfully evicted them. The tenants claimed that they paid rent in cash, but the landlord failed to keep good records. The tenant sued for the value of the property that had been dumped on the street and ruined during the eviction.

"It seems to me that both sides need to give a little," Judge Pohler began as the attorneys in front of her admired the décor of her chambers.

"My client has been completely reasonable. She is a landlord and is entitled to be paid. The tenants have no proof of payment for three months of rent. It's true that my client should have filed for an eviction instead of throwing stuff out on the street, but they were frustrated. Now these two are trying to sue us? Do you really believe that the Chases had twenty thousand dollars worth of property in their apartment?" Cornelius fired.

"Mr. Chase *says* that he was current with the rent. He *says* that he paid in cash. I'll just leave it at that," Brittany said without offering anything else that her client had told her. She did not believe her clients. Mr. Chase argued vehemently in their initial consultation that his landlord required cash payments because he did not trust checks from Section 8 tenants or anyone receiving public assistance.

Judge Pohler advised Brittany to counsel the Chases into dismissing their claim and to pay one month of rent as a compromise or face a heavy judgment and attorneys' fees. Brittany agreed with the judge and shook hands with opposing counsel as the two exited chambers.

"This doesn't make sense. We paid rent. The landlord broke the law by throwing out our stuff. We lost everything! Did you talk to the other tenants? No one was allowed to pay with checks," Mr. Chase argued. Brittany stuck to her guns and strongly advised her clients to pay one month of rent and to move on since they had no proof of their cash payments. The Chases relented and made the payment.

Seven months later, Brittany received a call from Tera McClaude, another tenant who had been evicted from Lenzaw Ridge Apartments. She also claimed to have made cash payments and that she had audio recordings from her mobile phone of each payment since the landlord refused to provide receipts.

Unlike Brittany's mishandling of *Chase vs Lenzaw Ridge Apartments*, the attorney visited the apartment complex and interviewed other tenants. Tenant after tenant informed the attorney that they were required to pay in cash as well and that the landlord refused to provide receipts.

Brittany felt horribly for not believing the Chases enough to gather witnesses before trial. Brittany felt even worse for not speaking up for the Chases in front of Judge Pohler and opposing counsel. If she had faith in them, she would have verified their story and she would have stood up for them.

In 2 Corinthians 4:13-14, Paul says: "It is written: "I believed; therefore I have spoken." Since we have that same spirit of faith, we also believe and therefore speak." There is a tremendous difference between being an introvert and being a doubter. Silence is often evidence of a lack of faith. Brittany did not believe her clients; therefore, she did not speak up for them. She had no faith in them or their cause. She conceded defeat without a fight.

The *Spirit of faith* opens our mouths to proclaim the gospel of Christ and the love of the Father. If Christians truly believe in scripture, they must confess it not only for their freedom and salvation, but for the freedom and salvation of others. Imagine how disappointed the Chases felt in having an attorney who did not believe in them enough to speak up for them. Imagine how disappointed our Lord must be when Christians do not believe in Him enough to speak up and profess their faith. The Church displays the same weakness, the same compromise, and the same disloyalty as Brittany when it fails to act as bold ambassadors for Christ Jesus.

CROSS EXAMINATION – *Examined by the Cross*

1. *Has the Spirit of faith been evidenced by your words?*
2. *Can you honestly say, "I believed; therefore I have spoken?"*
3. *Have you ever been in the Chases' position and had someone fail to speak up and fight for you?*
4. *Have you ever been in Brittany's position and regretted not having spoken up for someone or about something?*
5. *Pray today for greater faith, greater conviction, and greater courage to speak up whenever your voice is needed to advance the kingdom of God.*

"No man is better for knowing that God so loved the world of men
that He gave His only begotten son to die for their redemption.
In hell there are millions who know that.
Theological truth is useless until it is obeyed.
The purpose behind all doctrine is to secure moral action."
A. W. Tozer

Day 88

Spirit Of Love

"If I speak in the tongues of men and of angels,
but have not love, I am only a resounding gong
or a clanging cymbal.
If I have the gift of prophecy and can fathom
all mysteries and all knowledge,
and if I have a faith that can move mountains,
but have not love, I am nothing.
If I give all I possess to the poor
and surrender my body to the flames,
but have not love, I gain nothing."
1 Corinthians 13:1-3 - NIV

"I'm not going to get into Monday morning quarterbacking with you. No lawyer would have cut you the breaks that I gave you. I didn't charge you for half the stuff that I did. Let's just move on from here!" Leonard yelled in the corridor of the court building. He had taken on a hazardous workplace claim on behalf of a factory worker suffering severe respiratory problems.

"You asked me how I felt and I gave you an honest answer. You did a great job in presenting our case; I just think you let their expert witness off easy when you cross examined him," stated Kay.

"What are you talking about?" asked Leonard.

"You didn't ask any follow up questions when he started lying about his training and knowledge of environmental standards. I gave you a copy of the federal regulations and a copy of company standards. They weren't in compliance. His testimony made things sound optional. I'm not saying you did a bad job overall, but you dropped the ball in a few places so the case is now closer than it should be," Kay explained.

Leonard had just spent a full day litigating and did not have the stamina to argue with a client. He had made many sacrifices to help Kay. Leonard had significantly under-billed his whistle blowing client and believed he deserved a pat on the back instead of criticism. However, Leonard had to admit to himself that he cut corners in the weeks leading up to the trial. Leonard had worked the case diligently for 75% of the time, but failed to put in the hours that the case required towards the end and it showed.

Pride overtook Leonard in these moments. He felt that Kay should have been grateful to have an attorney in a nice firm take his case. *"No one would have taken this case for this pay,"* Leonard thought. As Leonard contemplated sending a hefty and more accurate final legal invoice to his critiquing "ungrateful" client, he noticed the What Would Jesus Do bracelet on her wrist.

Jesus died for his clients even when they did not appreciate Him. He argued a case for the salvation of a sin sick human race. Although Jesus had done nothing wrong, he had been betrayed, denied, spat upon, humiliated, beaten, and killed. Unlike Jesus, Leonard's sacrifice for Kay had been greatly flawed. Leonard's good deeds held no value. He had to admit that there was no love in his actions over the last few months. He acted as if he had done Kay a favor and as if no one had the right to question him. Leonard quickly sent an invoice which contained an apology and a zero balance. He opted not to charge his client for the last month of service because he saw no value in work that was not done in love.

The apostle Paul defined "love" in 1 Corinthians 13, but he also provided a good description of Jesus Christ. We know that Jesus is love, so if we replace the word with the name that is above all names we see a greater dimension of love.

"~~Love~~ Jesus is patient, ~~love~~ Jesus is kind. ~~It~~ Jesus does not envy, ~~it~~ Jesus does not boast, ~~it~~ Jesus is not proud. ~~It~~ Jesus is not rude, ~~it~~ Jesus is not self-seeking, ~~it~~ Jesus is not easily angered, ~~it~~ Jesus keeps no record of wrongs. ~~Love~~ Jesus does not delight in evil but rejoices with the truth. ~~It~~ Jesus always protects, always trusts, always hopes, always perseveres. ~~Love~~ Jesus never fails. But where there are prophecies, they will cease; where there are tongues, they will be stilled; where there is knowledge, it will pass away."

1 Corinthians 13:4-8 NIV – edited for emphasis

CROSS EXAMINATION – *Examined by the Cross*

1. Do you believe the absence of love invalidates a good deed?
2. Have you ever had someone do a great thing for you, but it felt meaningless because there was no love in it?
3. Have you ever done something for someone and been told that it was meaningless because your heart wasn't in it?
4. Does Barbara have the right to criticize a person who is doing her a favor?

"I won't just look for a miracle;
I will become someone's miracle
by showing God's love and mercy wherever I go.
This is my declaration."
Joel Osteen

Day 89

SPIRIT OF GLORY

**"If you are insulted because of the name of Christ,
you are blessed,
for the Spirit of glory
and of God rests on you."**
1 Peter 4:14 - NIV

Iris managed to hold back the tears as she thanked the judge for the mercy that he had granted her client. Instead of sending Regina Samuels to juvenile detention for a year, he required her to perform forty hours of community service, attend personal counseling sessions, and to check in with a probation officer for the next ten months. Regina could not hold back her tears and cried openly. Judge Hawthorne immediately received confirmation that he had made the correct decision to give the young defendant another chance.

Iris had dedicated an unusual amount of time mentoring the young lady and helping her to see the error in trying to steal a car. Iris had even secured a part time job for Regina to help her make restitution to the owner of the car and to install a work ethic in the troubled youth.

"Regina, the judge gave you grace. God gives all of us a second chance. I know you're destined to do great things," Iris said as she gave her client a final hug.

"You don't get tired of preaching do you?" snapped Kurt as he pulled his daughter, Regina, away from the attorney. Iris could not understand what had changed in Kurt. This was a happy day. Their prayers had been answered. Iris clearly remembered the day in church when Kurt first tapped her on the back. Kurt cried that his daughter had gotten involved with the wrong crowd and faced jail time.

Iris worked the case at no charge and succeeded on every level. Initially, the State tried Regina as an adult and sought jail time. The skilled defense attorney convinced the State to try her as a juvenile. Iris, then, convinced the court to consider Regina's traumatic experiences as a child who saw her mother's death in a car accident. The judge responded to the pleas with probation and community service. Iris expected Kurt to be ecstatic, yet she suddenly encountered an intense anger and hatred.

"You helped her, but you don't have to be so self-righteous and throw things in her face. Next, you'll want people bowing down to you!" Kurt yelled as the attorney scooped papers into her briefcase.

Regina tried to apologize for her father, but Iris quietly retreated and left the courthouse. Iris slammed her car door and began to think of all the hateful things that she should have said to Kurt.

"Don't get mad at me because I kept your daughter out of jail. It's not my fault that you weren't a good example for her!" Iris mouthed. The bruised attorney prayed for forgiveness for saying and thinking such horrible things. Iris prayed for Kurt and for an understanding of why her friend from church had suddenly become an enemy.

Within moments, Iris received the answer from the Holy Spirit. Kurt had become enslaved to a spirit of jealousy and pride. Kurt appreciated Iris when he feared the worse from the criminal justice system; however, the moment that the punishment had been avoided Kurt's true prideful nature surfaced. He was embarrassed for needing Iris. He was ashamed for not having the money to pay Iris. He even feared that Iris or other members of the church would look down on him and his family. Kurt also hated the fact that Regina viewed Iris as more of a role model than her own father.

The Holy Spirit revealed that Iris had no reason to be surprised by Kurt's resentment. Believers in Christ Jesus carry the Spirit of Glory. The world will resent the excellence within the children of God and God's favor. True Christians are not self-righteous goodie goodies, they are simply people trying to walk within the standard that God has established.

The Spirit of Glory calls us to a great standard, to a great throne, but also to great persecution. We are the envy of the world.

CROSS EXAMINATION – *Examined by the Cross*

1. *Can you identify one Christian in whom you see the Spirit of Glory?*
2. *Do you see the Spirit of Glory in yourself?*
3. *Do other people see the Spirit of Glory within you?*
4. *Have you ever been persecuted because of the standard within you that has been set by the Spirit of Glory?*
5. *How is it possible that someone can admire you, ask you for help, and then resent you for helping?*
6. *Why is it futile for someone to try to diminish the Spirit of Glory? What does envy do to the envious?*

"A saint is a person so grasped by a religious vision that it becomes central to his or her life in a way that radically changes the person and leads others to glimpse the value of that vision."
Dietrich Bonhoeffer

Day 90

Spirit of Invitation

> "The Spirit and the bride say, "Come!"
> And let him who hears say, "Come!"
> Whoever is thirsty, let him come;
> and whoever wishes, let him take the free gift
> of the water of life."
> **Revelation 22:17 - NIV**

The Bible is filled with invitations from God to His people. The Lord invited: Adam to life without death in the garden[18]; childless Abram to become Abraham, the father of a nation[19]; Moses to lead the enslaved out of slavery[20]; Samuel to be His voice[21]; David, through a prophet, to become a king and powerful bloodline[22]; Jonah to preach to Nineveh; the disciples to become fishers of men[23]; and invited you to open the door where He stands and knocks.[24]

---

[18] **Genesis 2:16-17**

[19] **Genesis 12:1-3**

[20] **Exodus 3:10**

[21] **1 Samuel**

[22] **1 Samuel 16:12-13**

[23] **Matthew 4:18-22**

[24] **Revelation 3:20**

Throughout the book of Revelation, the Spirit of the Lord invites the people of God to choose life over death and fellowship over separation. The Spirit extended individual invitations to the seven churches while constantly asking all who have ears to hear to listen and to act.

To the Church in Ephesus:

"He who has an ear, let him hear what the Spirit says to the churches.
To him who overcomes, I will give the right to eat from the tree of life, which is in the paradise of God."
Revelation 2:7 – NIV emphasis added

To the Church in Smyrna:

"He who has an ear, let him hear what the Spirit says to the churches.
He who overcomes will not be hurt at all by the second death."
Revelation 2:11 – NIV emphasis added

To the Church in Pergamum:

"He who has an ear, let him hear what the Spirit says to the churches.
To him who overcomes, I will give some of the hidden manna.
I will also give him a white stone with a new name written on it, known only to the one who receives it."
Revelation 2:17 – NIV emphasis added

To the Church in Tyra:

"He who has an ear, let him hear what the Spirit says to the churches."
Revelation 2:29 NIV emphasis added

To the Church in Sardis:

"He who has an ear, let him hear what the Spirit says to the churches."
Revelation 3:6 NIV emphasis added

To the Church in Philadelphia:

"He who has an ear, let him hear what the Spirit says to the churches."
Revelation 3:13 - NIV emphasis added

To the Church in Laodicea:

"To him who overcomes,
I will give the right to sit with me on my throne, just as I overcame and sat down with my Father on his throne.
*He who has an ear, let him hear what
the Spirit says to the churches.'"*
Revelation 3:21-22 – NIV emphasis added

The true revelation in the Book of Revelation is the revelation of Christ Jesus. All are invited to eternal life with the King of Kings and Lord of Lords as he takes His rightful throne over all evil and wickedness. Christians are invited to accept Him on the thrones of their hearts in exchange for sharing a throne with Him throughout eternity.

This devotional is a personal invitation to love the Lord with all of your heart, your soul, and your mind. I invite you to pursue the Living Fountain and to thirst no more. My invitation allows for plus one, plus one thousand, and even plus one billion, so please extend it to others.

The Spirit of the Lord is an inviting Spirit who cries out to the lost, to the hurting, to the confused, and to the weak to receive love. *Let all who have ears to hear, hear what the Spirit is saying. Come!*

CROSS EXAMINATION - *Examined by the Cross*

1. *What invitation has God extended to you whether stated in the Bible or stated to you directly in your spirit?*
2. *How have you responded to the invitation?*
3. *Have you invited others through the sharing of the gospel?*
4. *Will you share this devotional with others and invite them into a victorious life on earth and into an eternal life thereafter?   Yes / No*

"How happy is such a soul that has not only the voice behind
him saying, 'This is the way, walk in it;'
but also the witness within him that the voice is divine,
and telling him of the end,
which by that way he may attain!"
Richard Baxter

Quote Sources

Page 16

"Two cities have been formed by two loves: the earthly city by the love of self, leading to contempt of God and the heavenly city by the love of God, leading to contempt of self. The former glorifies in itself, the latter in the Lord. . .These cities are the communities of men."

St. Augustine

Source:
Lane, Thomas, *A Concise History of Christian Thought*,
(Michigan, Baker Academic: 2006) pg 53

Page 20

"Let us remove the ignorance and darkness that spreads like a mist over our sight, and let us get a vision of the true God."

Clement of Alexandria

Source:
Galli, Mark and Olsen, Ted ed. *131 Christians Everyone Should Know*,
(Tennessee, Holman Reference: 2000) p52

Page 23

"But to take God's name in vain is not just a matter of words –it's also about thoughts and deeds. . .To call God "Lord" and disobey him is to take his name in vain. To call God "Father" and be filled with anxiety and doubts is to deny his name."

John Stott

Source:
Stott, John, *Basic Christianity*
(Michigan, William B Eerdmans Publishing Co.: 2008) p 80

Page 26

"And God in his goodness has called us to live out the Christian life together, as our mutual love and care reflect the love and care of God.
Relationships imply commitment in the world. Surely they imply no less in the church.
He never meant our growth to occur alone on an island but with and through one another."

Mark Dever

Source:
Dever, Mark, *What Is a Healthy Church?*
(Illinois, Crossway Books: 2007) pg 122

Page 38

> "Sin will always take you further than you wanted to go
> and cost you more than you wanted to pay."
> Tony Evans

Source:
Evans, Tony, *Life Essentials*
(Chicago, Moody Publishers: 2003) pg 211

Page 42

> "When our deepest desire is not the things of God, or a favor from God,
> but God Himself, we cross a threshold."
> Max Lucado

Source:
Lucado, Max, *It's Not About Me*
(Tennessee, Integrity Publishings: 2004) pg 17

Page 54

> "Never forget that God is able to lift you from fatigue of despair to the buoyancy of hope, and
> transform dark and desolate valleys into sunlit paths of inner peace."
> Rev. Dr. Martin Luther King, Jr.

Source:
Carson, Clayborne ed. *A Time to Break Silence: The Essential Works of Martin
Luther King, Jr. for Students* (Boston, Beacon Press: 1994) pg 197

Page 58

> "If we are not feeding on the Word, we are not walking after the Spirit,
> and we will not have victory over the flesh and over sin."
> Robert Torrey

Source:
Torrey, R.A. *The Presence and Work of the Holy Spirit,*
(Pennsylvania, Whitaker House: 1996) pg 115

Page 62

> "A man groping in darkness doesn't need a lesson on darkness;
> he needs light. That light is Jesus."
> Hazem Farraj

Source:

Farraj, Hazem, *Mohammed, Jesus & Me*
(California, Reflections Publishing: 2013) pg 117

Page 68

> "This is the open secret of how to live as a Christian.
> It is not about us struggling in vain to be more like Jesus,
> but allowing him, by the power of his Spirit,
> to come and change us from the inside.
> Once again, we see that to have him as our example is not enough;
> we need him as our Savior."
> John Stott

Source:

Stott, John, *Basic Christianity*
(Michigan, William B Eerdmans Publishing Co.: 2008) pg 123

Page 72

> "The Church's approach to an intelligent carpenter is usually confined to exhorting him not
> to be drunk and disorderly in his leisure hours, and to come to church on Sundays.
> What the Church should be telling him is this: that the very first demand that his religion
> makes upon him is that he should make good tables."
> Dorothy Sayers

Source:
Galli, Mark and Olsen, Ted ed. *131 Christians Everyone Should Know*,
(Tennessee, Holman Reference: 2000) p 131

Page 75

> "The Living Water offered me
> Was cool and quenched my thirst.
> In return He wanted me
> To only put Him first."
> Jeanie Niemoller

Source:
Niemoller, Jeannie *Glimpses of His Awesome Glory*
(USA, Xlibris: 2012) pg 76

Page 79

"Jesus is all. When He judges, He is Law; when He teaches, He is Word; when He saves, He is Grace; when He begets, He is Father; when begotten He is Son; when He suffers, He is Lamb; when buried, He is Man; when risen, He is God. Such is Jesus Christ! To Him be glory forever, amen!"
Melito, Bishop of Sardis

Source:
Schmitt, Charles P. *Floods Upon the Dry Ground,*
(Pennsylvania, Destiny Image Publishers: 1988) pg 31

Page 82

Pope Innocent IV: You see, the day is past when the church could say, "Silver and gold have I none."

Thomas Aquinas: Yes, Holy Father. . . and the day is past when the church could say to the lame man, "Rise and walk!"

Source:
Schmitt, Charles P. *Floods Upon the Dry Ground,*
(Pennsylvania, Destiny Image Publishers: 1988) pgs 87-88 citing
John W. Kennedy, The Torch of the Testimony (Gospel Literature Service, 1965; Goleta, CA: Christian Books, reprint) pg 122

Page 85

"Disappointments are inevitable, but discouragement is a choice."
Charles Stanley

Source:
Stanley, Charles   *Emotions*
(New York, Howard Books: 2013) pg 235

Page 100

"But if the church will free itself from the shackles of a deadening status quo and recovering its great historic mission, will speak and act fearlessly and insistently in terms of justice and peace, it will enkindle the imagination of mankind and fire the souls of men, imbuing them with a glowing and ardent love for truth, justice and peace."
Rev. Dr. Martin Luther King, Jr.

Source:
Carson, Clayborne and Holloran, Peter ed.   *A Knock at Midnight*
(New York, Warner Brothers, Inc.: 1998) pg 73

Page 111

"Rebounding should never mean forcing up another bad shot.
It should mean creating the opportunity for a new and improved shot."
Vera Jones

Source:
Jones, Vera   *Play Through The Foul*
(Florida, VoiceWork's Media: 2009) pg 116

Page 119

"There is a holiness about your tears.
Each one is a prayer that only God can understand.
He created them and shed them Himself.
They are His reminder to you that your soul can have
no rainbows,
if your eyes can have no tears."
Kathe Wunnenberg

Source:
Wunnenberg, Kathe   *Grieving the Loss of a Loved One*
(Michigan, Zondervan Publishing House: 2000) pg 91

Page 132

*"Love has a hem to her garment
That reaches the very dust.
It sweeps the stains
From the streets and lanes,
And because it can, it must."*
Mother Teresa

Source:
Benenate, Becky and Durepose, Joseph   *Mother Teresa - No Greater Love*
(California, New World Library: 1989)

Page 135

"Some people bless you when they come into your life;
some people bless you when they exit your life."
Jentezen Franklin

Source:
Franklin, Jentezen   *Right People, Right Place, Right Plan*
(Pennsylvania, Whitaker House: 2007) pg 135

<u>Page 139</u>

"All our words will be useless unless they come from within.
Words that do not give the light of Christ increase the darkness."
Mother Teresa

Source:
Benenate, Becky and Durepose, Joseph   *Mother Teresa - No Greater Love*
(California, New World Library: 1989) pg 16

<u>Page 153</u>

"I'm against sin. I'll kick it as long as I have a foot. I'll fight it as long as I have a fist. I'll butt
it as long as I have a head. I'll bite it as long as I've got a tooth. And when I'm old and
fistless and footless and toothless,
I'll gum it till I go home to Glory
and it goes home to perdition."
Billy Sunday

Source:
Galli, Mark and Olsen, Ted ed. *131 Christians Everyone Should Know,*
(Tennessee, Holman Reference: 2000) pg75

<u>Page 164</u>

"I preached. . .as a dying man to dying men."
Richard Baxter

Source:
Galli, Mark and Olsen, Ted ed. *131 Christians Everyone Should Know,*
(Tennessee, Holman Reference: 2000) pg 86

<u>Page 168</u>

"Wherever God is, there is Heaven."
St. Teresa of Avila

Source:
Ellsberg, *Robert   The Saints Guide to Happiness*
(New York, North Point Press: 2003) pg 184

Page 174

"We can hear children singing:
In Christ there is no East or West.
In Him no North or South,
But one great Fellowship of Love
Throughout the whole wide world.
This is the only way."
Rev. Dr. Martin Luther King, Jr.

Source:
Carson, Clayborne ed. *A Time to Break Silence: The Essential Works of Martin Luther King, Jr. for Students* (Boston, Beacon Press: 1994) pg 28

Page 179

"Ask God for His guidance;
once you get the nod of God on your decisions,
everything else will fall into place."
Jentezen Franklin

Source:
Franklin, Jentezen *Right People, Right Place, Right Plan* (Pennsylvania, Whitaker House: 2007) pgs 44-45

Page 184

"Christians display to us their wonderful and confessedly striking method of life. . . Every foreign land is to them as home, yet their every homeland is foreign. They pass their days on earth, but they are citizens of heaven. They obey the laws of the land, and at the same time surpass the law by their lives.
They love all and are reviled by all."
Anonymous

Source:
Schmitt, Charles P. *Floods Upon the Dry Ground,* (Pennsylvania, Destiny Image Publishers: 1988) pg 30

Page 190

"Poverty is freedom. It is a freedom so that what I possess doesn't own me, so that what I possess doesn't hold me down, so that my possessions don't keep me from sharing or giving of myself. Rigorous poverty is our safeguard."
Mother Teresa

Source:
Benenate, Becky and Durepose, Joseph *Mother Teresa - No Greater Love* (California, New World Library: 1989) pgs 96-97

Page 199

"I lived every day with the threat of death and I came to see many years ago that I couldn't function if I allowed fear to overcome me. The main thing is not how long I live, but how well I have acquitted myself in the discharge of these truths that are high, noble, and good."
Rev. Dr. Martin Luther King, Jr.

Source:
Ellsberg, Robert *The Saints Guide to Happiness*
(New York, North Point Press: 2003) pg 158

Page 202

"Notice that the mercy seat is placed over the law.
This tells us that God's mercy triumphs over judgment!"
Joseph Prince

Source:
Prince, Joseph *Destined to Reign*
(Oklahoma, Harrison House: 1982) pg 211

Page 213

"If you are poor in spirit, his kingdom He gives you. If you mourn, comfort He offers you. If you are meek, inheritance He leaves you. If you hunger and thirst for righteousness,
He will fill you.
If you're merciful, mercy He gives you.
If you're pure in heart, His face he shows you.
If you're a peacemaker, His son he names you. . ."
Hazem Farraj

Source:
Farraj, Hazem, *Mohammed, Jesus & Me*
(California, Reflections Publishing: 2013) pg 122

Page 217

"Thus it begins; the cross is not the terrible end to an otherwise
God-fearing and happy life,
but it meets us at the beginning of our communion with Christ.
When Christ calls a man, he bids him come and die."
Dietrich Bonhoeffer

Source:
Ellsberg, Robert *The Saints Guide to Happiness*
(New York, North Point Press: 2003) pg 142

Page 206

> "Our whole business in this life is to restore to health the eyes of the heart,
> whereby God may be seen."
> St. Augustine

Source:
Ellsberg, Robert *The Saints Guide to Happiness*
(New York, North Point Press: 2003) pg 171

Page 225

> "Deception is Satan's number one weapon,
> and discernment is our number one defense."
> Jentezen Franklin

Source:
Franklin, Jentezen *Right People, Right Place, Right Plan*
(Pennsylvania, Whitaker House: 2007) pg 155

Page 228

> "My thoughts are guided by God's Word every day. No obstacle can defeat me, because my
> mind is programmed for victory. This is my declaration."
> Joel Osteen

Source:
Osteen, Joel *I Declare: 31 Promises to Speak Over Your Life*
(New York, FaithWords: 2012) pg 81

Page 239

> "Whoever will become a preacher must feel the needs of men until it becomes
> an oppression to his soul."
> Leslie J. Tizard

Source:
Robinson, Haddon W.   *Biblical Preaching*
(Michigan, Baker Academic: 2001) pg 170

Page 243

"Prayer has brought hearing to the deaf, sight to the blind, life to the dead, salvation to the lost, and healing to the sick. Prevailing prayer should be the main business of our day."
Jentezen Franklin

Source:
Franklin, Jentezen *Right People, Right Place, Right Plan*
(Pennsylvania, Whitaker House: 2007) pg 113

Page 247

August Spangenberg:	Do you know Jesus Christ?
John Wesley:	I know He is the Savior of the world?
August Spangenberg:	True, but do you know He has saved you?

Schmitt, Charles P. *Floods Upon the Dry Ground,*
(Pennsylvania, Destiny Image Publishers: 1988) pg 127

Page 250

"Now at last we can say the Lord's Prayer without hypocrisy.
Previously the words had a rather hollow sound; now they ring with new and wonderful meaning. God is indeed our Father in heaven,
who knows our needs before we ask and
will not fail to give good things to his children."
John Stott

Source:
Stott, John, *Basic Christianity*
(Michigan, William B Eerdmans Publishing Co.: 2008) pg 157

Page 255

"If there is a need, He supplies it. If there is a wound, He cures it.
If there is a doubt, He destroys it."
Hazem Farraj

Source:
Farraj, Hazem, *Mohammed, Jesus & Me*
(California, Reflections Publishing: 2013) pg 122

Page 258

"A church is nothing better than an ethical club if its sympathies for lost souls do not overflow, and it does not go out to seek to point lost souls to the knowledge of Jesus Christ."
George W. Truett

Source:
Dever, Mark, *What Is a Healthy Church?*
(Illinois, Crossway Books: 2007) pg 77

Page 261

"And that is why, at the end of all things, when the sun rises here and the twilight turns to blackness down there, the Blessed will say 'We have never lived anywhere except in Heaven,' and the Lost, 'We were always in Hell.' And both will speak truly.
but forgetting that one day he will."
C. S. Lewis

Source:
Klein, Patricia A.   ed. *A Year With C.S. Lewis*, edited by Patricia S. Klein
(New York, Harper One: 2003) pg 320

Page 264

"Communion is that state where man seeks to live in the will of God, the wonder of God. Communion necessitates that two must covenant themselves, two must agree. Communion is that power which comes to a person whose life really pleases the Lord. Wherever there is communion there is power."
Rev. Dr. Harold A. Carter

Source:
Carter, Harold A. *The Preaching of Jonah*
(Illinois, Progressive Baptist Publishing House: 1981) pg 58

Page 270

"God gives you the strength to press
against the pressure that's pressing you!"
Joyce Meyers

Source:
Meyers, Joyce *You Can Begin Again*
(New York, FaithWords: 2014) pg 99

Page 274

"Cheap grace is preaching forgiveness without requiring repentance, baptism without church discipline, communion without confession. . . Cheap grace is grace without discipleship, grace without the cross, grace without Jesus Christ, living and incarnate."
Dietrich Bonhoeffer

Source:
Galli, Mark and Olsen, Ted ed. *131 Christians Everyone Should Know*,
(Tennessee, Holman Reference: 2000) pg 378

Page 278

"Eighty-six years have I served Him, and He has done me no wrong: how then can I blaspheme my Savior and King?"
Polycarp

Source:
Schmitt, Charles P. *Floods Upon the Dry Ground*,
(Pennsylvania, Destiny Image Publishers: 1988) pg 24

Page 287

"God never calls a person without giving that person a specific assignment, a place to carry out the assignment, and the amazing grace in which to complete the mission."
Rev. Dr. Harold A. Carter

Source:
Carter, Harold A. *The Preaching of Jonah*,
(Illinois, Progressive Baptist Publishing House: 1981) pg58

Page 296

"Reducing the human job description down to one phrase, and this is it: reflect God's glory."
Max Lucado

Source:
Lucado, Max *It's Not about Me*
(Tennessee, Integrity Publishers: 2004) pgs 82-83

Page 302

"You cannot have peace as long as demons control your life. They will always lead you astray. They would direct your path away from God. When you are cleansed, you need the Holy Spirit to fill every corner of your life so that evil spirits have no place to dwell."
Mary Baxter

Source:
Baxter, Mary   *A Divine Revelation of the Spirit Realm*
(Pennsylvania, Whitaker House: 2000)

Page 309

"A *prophetic word* is a special inspired message or word that a person receives in his or her inner spirit after a season of fasting and extended prayer or, at times, through an inspired utterance from Scripture and occasionally confirmed by a vocal gift from another believer."
Perry Stone

Source:
Stone, Perry   *Exposing Satan's Playbook*
(Florida, Charisma House: 2012)

Page 313

"We must be willing to leave behind what we have come to know, that we may more fully comprehend what is yet to be known."
Bishop Monroe Saunders, Jr.

Source:
Saunders, Jr., Monroe   *A Journey to Faith*
(USA, Xulon Press: 2011) pg 96

Page 319

"Holiness does not consist in mystic speculations, enthusiastic fervors, or uncommanded austerities; it consists in thinking as God thinks and willing as God wills."
John Brown

Source:
Swindoll, Charles   *Man to Man*
(Michigan, Zondervan Publishing House: 1996) pg 291

Page 323

"Citizens are born into the earthly city by a nature spoiled by sin, but they are born into the heavenly city by grace freeing nature from sin."
St. Augustine

Source:
Lane, Thomas, *A Concise History of Christian Thought*,
(Michigan, Baker Academic: 2006) pg53

Page 328

"No man is better for knowing that God so loved the world of men
that He gave His only begotten son to die for their redemption.
In hell there are millions who know that. Theological truth is useless until it is obeyed.
The purpose behind all doctrine is to secure moral action."
A. W. Tozer

Source:
Robinson, Haddon W. *Biblical Preaching*
(Michigan, Baker Academic: 2001) pg 107

Page 332

"I won't just look for a miracle;
I will become someone's miracle by showing God's love and mercy wherever I go.
This is my declaration."
Joel Osteen

Source:
Osteen, Joel *I Declare: 31 Promises to Speak Over Your Life*
(New York, FaithWords: 2012) pg 87

Page 336

"A saint is a person so grasped by a religious vision that it becomes central to his or her life in a way that radically changes the person and leads others to glimpse the value of that vision."
Dietrich Bonhoeffer
Source:
Marty, Martin *Dietrich Bonhoeffer's Letters and Papers From Prison*
(New Jersey, Princeton University Press : 2011)

Page 340

"How happy is such a soul that has not only the voice behind him saying, 'This is the way, walk in it;' but also the witness within him that the voice is divine, and telling him of the end, which by that way he may attain!"
Richard Baxter

Source:
Bell, James Stuart ed. *From the Library of C.S. Lewis: Selections From Writers Who Influenced His Spiritual Journey* (Colorado, Shawbrooks: 2004)

ABOUT THE AUTHOR

Gregory D. Yancey, Esq. (hereinafter "Greg") was raised in the Baptist Church, was confirmed in the Lutheran Church, and serves in a non-denominational church to the glory of God. His Christian foundation rests on the prayers and walk of his parents, Ronald and Sheila Yancey. There was no devil or demon that could prevent Sheila Yancey from making sure that her sons knew Jesus Christ as Lord and Savior.

At an early age, Greg was profoundly affected by his father, Ronald Yancey's civil rights anecdotes and pursuit to become the first African American to graduate from the Georgia Institute of Technology. The stories stirred Greg's thirst and hunger for justice and equality. By kindergarten, Greg declared that he would change the world as an attorney and never looked back.

By God's grace, Greg graduated from the University of Maryland at College Park and the Georgetown University Law Center and accomplished his goal of obtaining a *juris doctor*. Although he now owns and operates The Fighting Lawyer, LLC law firm and enjoys being an advocate for the downtrodden, he finds his greatest fulfillment in having a relationship with Jesus Christ.

He has served the Lord as a: Drama Ministry leader; Legal Ministry leader; Youth Instructor; Children's Ministry volunteer; prison ministry volunteer; bible study leader; and Church security volunteer. In light of these experiences, Greg has felt the call of God to preach for quite some time and struggled with discerning where and how to begin. One night while lying in bed, Greg heard a whisper in his ear saying "Does someone have to die for you to get into the pulpit?" The next day, he received a shocking call that his aunt had passed.

Less shocking but even more life changing, his uncle asked him to speak at the funeral. After hearing Greg's words, Rev. Dr. Harold A. Carter, then presiding pastor at New Shiloh Baptist Church in Baltimore, Maryland requested a meeting and told Greg that he should be preaching.

Greg has been ordained by God to preach the word and currently serves the Lord at Immanuel's Church in Silver Spring, Maryland under Pastor Charles and Dotty Schmitt as one of the founders of the Legal Ministry and a leader of the Drama Ministry. He has been a frequent guest preacher of Rebirth Tabernacle of Glory under the tutelage of Pastor Myra Harris and hosts a webcast entitled, "The Divine Law" in which he compares God's law and man's law.

Greg's ministry and best work can be seen in his: beautiful wife, Jewell; stepdaughter, Cora; and son, Gregory. Through the trials of this Christian lawyer, God has truly given Greg life and life more abundantly.

Made in the USA
Las Vegas, NV
18 August 2021